TO BE READ IN 500 YEARS

Also by Albert Goldbarth

To Be Read in 500 Years

POEMS

Albert Goldbarth

Graywolf Press

Publication of this volume is made possible in part by a grant provided by the Minnesota State Arts Board, through an appropriation by the Minnesota State Legislature; a grant from the Wells Fargo Foundation Minnesota; and a grant from the National Endowment for the Arts, which believes that a great nation deserves great art. Significant support has also been provided by the Bush Foundation; Target; the McKnight Foundation; and other generous contributions from foundations, corporations, and individuals. To these organizations and individuals we offer our heartfelt thanks.

Published by Graywolf Press
250 Third Avenue North, Suite 600
Minneapolis, Minnesota 55401
All rights reserved.

www.graywolfpress.org

Published in the United States of America

ISBN 978-1-55597-525-8

2   4   6   8   9   7   5   3

Library of Congress Control Number: 2008941965

Cover design: Kyle G. Hunter

Cover art: Jack Gaughan. Used with permission of the Jack Gaughan Estate, phoebeagaughan@yahoo.com.

Acknowledgments

The poems in this collection originally appeared in the following journals, the editors of which have my ongoing gratitude—in many cases, for what is now decades of similar generosity.

Alaska Review: "I'm Nobody! Who Are You? Are You Nobody, Too?"
Beloit Poetry Journal: "The Craft Lecture . . ." and "Imperfect Knowledge"
Boulevard: "Convergences"
Crazyhorse: "The Singing" and "The Voices"
The Georgia Review: "Dignity," "Too Here," "Signed On," and "Tool"
The Gettysburg Review: "Reseen in This New Context," "Dial H for 'Hero,'" and "'. . . a museum, of sorts, for errors.'"
Great River Review: "Rereading Attempts at Poetry from My Earliest Teenage Years" and "Unformed"
Green Mountains Review: "If We Were Honest" and "Hard Pope"
Hotel Amerika: "Autobiography: Magic"
The Iowa Review: "The Blank"
The Kenyon Review: "In Another" and "Through the Elements"
Laurel Review: "Birds" and "The Mailbox"
Mid-American Review: "Almanac"
New Letters: "Stopping by Woods on a Snowy Evening," "Beauty," "The Everything Song," "Alimentary," and "In a Wireless World"
The New Yorker: "The Way"
Nightsun: "Drongo"
Notre Dame Review: "Into Blossom"
Ontario Review: "Where Babies Come From"
Parnassus: "Danielle Suite"
Pleiades: "'I taped a sign over the first sign'"
Poetry: "Marble-Sized Song," "He Has," "1400," "3.b. Digital / a. Baginal wall," "'An enormous electro-magnet is used to steal the world's electricity,'" and "To Be Read in 500 Years"
Poetry East: "How Simile Works"
Poetry Northwest: "The Arc"
River Styx: "Evan's Mother's Urine"

Southwest Review: "Those Early Years" and "The Sword"
TriQuarterly: "Channeling the Lord"
Virginia Quarterly Review: "Not Sumerian," "'The lions in his menagerie ate parrots,
  and he fed his horses grapes.'" and "Swallow"

"Stopping By Woods on a Snowy Evening" was reprinted in *The Best American Poetry 2007* (thanks to Heather McHugh).

"The Mailbox" also appeared as a limited edition art chapbook from Red Dragonfly Press (thanks to Scott King).

"Into Blossom" also appeared in *The Book,* a limited edition art chapbook from the New York Center for Book Arts (designed by Amber McMillan).

"To Be Read in 500 Years" and "Marble-Sized Song" were also included on the *Poetry Daily* web site (thanks to Don Selby and Diane Boller).

No computer was used in the creation or submission of these poems, and many of the journals above deserve extra thanks for their efforts during editing and production—as does the stalwart support team at Graywolf Press.

As always: these were written more happily because I live with Skyler.

With fond memories of Ray Smith's editorial acumen and charm.

And if I don't mention my sister Livia I'll never hear the end of it.

A buxom woman with pale green skin and flashing eyes hailed him from the open front of her establishment, where girls of different hues and at least three different shapes preened themselves.

"The ninety-nine joys dwell here, oh Earthmen! Enter!"

Dilullo shook his head. "Not I, mother. I crave the hundredth joy."

"And what is the hundredth joy?"

"The joy of sitting down quietly and reading a good book."

—EDMOND HAMILTON, *STARWOLF*

. . . so that human achievements may not be forgotten in time

—HERODOTUS
(TR. AUBREY DE SÉLINCOURT)

Contents

TOWARD (AND AGAINST) THE FUTURE

LOVE AND DEATH ON THE COSMIC ODOMETER: 1

Reseen in This New Context

"Lobster"—on a rabbi's table.
"Dirt" and "junk" are famous examples.
Things, become wrong simply
through displacement. "Bleeding"
—in its proper sphere it's "circulation."
—Mouse I once saw painfully pulling itself
(such mewling *must* mean pain) across
a carpet by its two front paws: the back ones
flat and mangled, and its guts being dragged behind it
like some bloody, undeployed parachute.

I've been a good reader of Donald Hall's poems,
as he's been a good (occasionally, a great) writer of poems
—and even so, through what I call his "late middle period"
(say, through 1988) I'm not sure either one of us
did justice to death. I say this even knowing him

to have always been, from the first, a Linnaeus
of categorizing death's profusions, a Rosa Parks
who wouldn't budge, who wouldn't yield his spot
on that bus in its long drive through the dark.
The birth of his son is a sign
the parents, "twenty-five and twenty-two," now
"start to die together." Of a "best friend" and his wife:
"in muscular bodies they walk to their deaths together."
Of neighbors. Of a sister. And "my mother's
painful hand that rubbed my father's head all night
as he lay dying." This awareness never ceases,
never turns its gaze away from "the repeated deaths
of preparation for death." And none of it cheaply wrought,
or of one lonely note: it isn't defiance of death,
nor is it capitulation, it doesn't attempt to appease.
It's candor, is what it is . . . an understanding of *our* place

in *its* place on the journey of lightwaves from aleph to omega.
And yet . . . I was so young when I first read so many of these,
and innocent (the more likable twin of ignorant).
Now, when I hear of his health in its failing—now,
when an extra quality I can only call "undeniable" or "irreducible"
enters the equation—I open his book and recite his
"Let us praise death in old age. Wagging our tails,
bowing, whimpering . . ." and it's suddenly intolerable,

those words, that poem, my howling I keep in my chest
like a child trapped inside an abandoned refrigerator,
it's intolerable, the idea of it, that mouse's bowel,
reseen in this new context.

⇒⇐

Of course it's also true that, sometimes, a recontext
will allow an admission of new and unforeseeable wonder.
The cover of my friend Dana's new book
is the nose [the snout?] of a shark, in close-up zoom
that has it looking like . . . what? . . . some Neolithic temple,
two doors in a lumpen earthworks dome.
I like that sharp spin of 180 what-the-hell degrees.
But "wonder" isn't the tone of my mood today.
And so I find myself thinking back to that elderly man

—he's eighty-plus—who was honored last year
at a comic-con, as a master
of 1940s and 50s science fiction art. He stumbled up
to the podium, obviously gratified in a humble way
(he'd labored for so many decades in anonymity),
but also confused, and frail, and now his central labor
was breathing, itself: through two tubes
that attached to an oxygen canister
he had strapped to his back . . . this man

who'd created the future for me, in 1958, when I was ten,
a world of cleanly-lineated spired cities on other planets
in the year 3000 A.D., and my mother was still alive,
she was young and fiercely alive and the day was fresh
in her strong nose and along her forest of hair,
and the citizenry of Marsport steered their zip-cars
through the air, and robots attended them,
and my father was still alive, "we're a little *meshuggeh,*
but boy we have fun," he taught me how to open a too-tight lid
and what to say to the neighbors, and spaceships
(lord, how that man could draw spaceships!) sleeked
like aluminum tropical fish among the moons,
and my sister was five, before the lump, before
her husband's swift MS, and a hero, an honest space hero,
was shooting out of the atmosphere
with a bubble helmet of oxygen on his head
and a blast-pack canister on his back that trailed
a long safe flame of atomic glory behind him.

If We Were Honest

When I tell you that cultural ritual is an artifice
composed of simultaneous chrono-vectors,
I'm thinking of sex. I mean it.
We all are. It isn't just me. Or when I say
the war, or the god, or the list with the juice and the cereal . . .
sex. What is it the psycho-experts are claiming?—every ten seconds?
When I tell you that I'm thinking of sex,

I'm thinking of death. Its worm is always
in my eye, its sour and dirt-blown web is always
a catch in my throat. It was always a wen
releasing a small electrical jolt to the brain
of Napoleon, Alexander, Attila. It was funereally
in the black, black ink of the Brontës;
why should I be any different? Why can't we

be honest?—every poem is "Sex." (Or "Death.")
If we were honest, half of our poems would be about
the making of poems, the conference on the making of poems,
the resumé of poems successfully made . . . you know, the way
that half of our time is actually spent. And did
ten seconds pass just now? If so, then
sex. (If so, then death.) Not too long after

the *Dolphin* first made port in Tahiti, it was discovered
the crew were trading its nails
for dalliances with the pliant and welcoming
women of that island—"to such a great extent, the ship
was in danger of being pulled apart."
Inside the cradling waves of moonlight
on those waters . . . smiling . . . consummating . . . human

nails into smooth, bamboo-brown human grain . . .
how did they know, how could they foresee, that
my mother would die from her own lungs
shaping hundreds of obstinate fists in her chest,
my father would die with his own blood turning
into a useless negative of itself?
And yet they must have known, they must have seen the lesson,

they were trying to deny it with the drive of such
combustive, zealous engines! This is my topic
tonight, and how the craft of poetry and the role
of the postmodern yes a bare knee like a beacon,
like a skull beneath the face-skin, and a question
from the audience is yes in my mind, yes in yours, yes
sex and death—the one thing.

The Singing

"Pickleheads with insect eyes," a friend describes
the green men out of saucer fandom: thousands gather annually
to parse their fanatical credulousness. I don't
believe some otherplanet sapience in celadon iguana skin
exists, much less is manifest on Earth (and thus implicitly
contributes its ophidian or photosynthetic consciousness to the layer
of Gaean cerebration-essences that, ever since we branched off
from the long line of progenitor life-forms, circles overhead).
And yet . . . who hasn't, in between our island moments
of rationality, felt . . . a weightedness, a . . . presence, yes,
a presence in the air, that might imply the astonishing visit
of . . . something, yes, of something so beyond the language's ability
to offer us accommodating images, we might as well
say "extragalactic" and buy up the little green keychains.

—⁂—

Angels? . . . no. They fall outside my recognition system
by the width of about a billion UOL's (that's Units of Logic), both
the furrow-visaged wielders of flaming, prohibitive swords *and*
all those dewy, pastry-bodied, wingéd flitterers so prevalent
on greeting cards. Soothsayers . . . stigmatics . . . telekinetics . . .
no. Although what to make of my friend the widow

at 28 who, after a year of ash and lonely grieving, came back
into the world again and met a man at the library, "there
were sparks," and she could sense, could *know,* her husband was
observing and approved, she could feel his breath
and roused awareness, she could feel his generous nod, and when
one night at last this man undressed her, she could feel
her husband cup her hips to help her thrust her sex up wildly
to meet him. Who am I to say no?

⇒ ⇐

Frankly, if *I* die first I'd like my wife to mourn
from the roan of her bountiful hair down
to the cellular level every day, and make of this a living testimony
that precludes another man. She said she'd try
to comply, although I thought I saw some errant sparkle
of withholding in her eye. In any case, I find her
a comfort. She was with me on the porch that day
the two cops with the swab kit came to call—because
I fit the age, and the race, and the relevant zip codes,
and I have (as colleague X once said) "an offensively
salty mouth": which I now gaped for them,
to yield its pink to their investigations. "Oh—and
will these samples be destroyed?" she asked. *I* hadn't thought
to think of saliva in terms of its afterlife.

⇒ ⇐

I don't believe in them, though you might
—ghosts. If so, perhaps you'll know the level
at which a spectral persistence begins. Does the heart contain
its own lingering phantom-self? does blood?
does DNA? If it's a blueprint for the whole of us, then
surely DNA contains a blueprint of our ghost, and it
will be released, at the time of release, with the rest of us,

into the energy-can-neither-be-created-nor-destroyedosphere,
into the thoughtiverse. I've fancied if we had the proper nets
to swing around, then we might capture an occasional lavish bee
of sheer cognition as it's homing for the hive. Of if we had
the proper ears, then we might hear the final singing
as the Wichita police deliver this first of us
and last of us to the flames of incineration.

The Arc

"*. . . the beautifully written roll containing the second book of the* Iliad
*that archeologists discovered placed under the head of the mummy of a
woman.*"

—LIONEL CASSON

It's not the trees in Ovid's *Metamorphoses*
that earn our deepest wonder, not even the oak and the linden

that both grow from a single trunk; and not the perfect beauty
of Galatea, for which the wind itself is heard

to moan in longing, and the flowers bow their heads.
Not these; what really revs the engine

of our wonder is the arc, that starts
in dailiness: the lovers

who *become* those two trees, scaled-over and budded
into a unity for which their human selves

were the rehearsal; and the block of perfect marble
that was sculpted into Galatea's shape, and then translated

into life by the breath of the goddess Venus, seemingly
(in our later language) accurate to the chromosomes.

It's not the destination, it's the journey (bumper sticker
on an old friend's crazy, daisy-painted 70s VW van);

it isn't the flame, but the fact
that it was once just pure idea under the mineral lid

of a lump of coal. And so it wasn't my mother's death
that shocked us (after all, the cancer's steady alteration

of her lungs to two gray urns
was slow enough); it was the photograph we chanced on,

in a ragged fan of paper miscellany
from her bottom dresser drawer: a girl of fourteen

on the north shore of Lake Michigan . . . her arms out
to the sides as if they're brand-new wings she's modeling

for a mad inventor . . . hair blown back
in a matching aerodynamic banner, her fresh breasts

clearly flirting for their first time with the nubble
of her cotton shirt, and her nostrils very obviously,

greedily inhaling her two ribbons
of air from the Earth's unlimited spool of it, as if

this simple joy will never stop. It's what
the smarter stage magicians understand: the end

is more zip-pow astounding if its elephant is in
the pocket-lining of an ordinary overcoat,

its leotarded damsel is the genie of a common
aluminum canister. Despite their stunning immanence on stage,

it isn't the elephant or the svelte assistant:
it's the transformation. It's the epic poem

that, over time, becomes a pillow
wedged beneath a woman's skull. She must have loved it

ardently; she must have *loved* this little, private magic
into taking place. And we're *all* on the arc of a pilgrimage trail,

molecule by molecule becoming something different.
Presto Change-o says the conjurer, but anyone knows

the secret of that. It's easy enough to start
to make two lumps of coal: just close your eyes.

He Has

the high-boned taut-toned moody ink-eyes beauty
some men lead a girl to hell with whistling all the while.
Or say her every step displays the little jump-start jazz
in her ass that a boy's gaze superglues to, even over
broken glass, humiliation, fiscal ruin. The eye
betrays us daily. The eye, and the frame we bring
to our seeing. On the beach: that beautiful cartouche
of a raw-sienna feathering and pucker is—*step back*—
the fatal sear of a jellyfish whip across the chest
of one more luckless tourist. Try to tell her husband
how museum-worthy you find the design of her death.
Is the beauty the glutinous spiral of fish guts;
or the voluminous screw-thread spiraling-down of the gulls
to gorge? Proximity determines so much.
When you're twelve you dream of "going to war,"
and not of it coming to you.

Marble-Sized Song

Does she love you? *She* says yes, but really
how do you *know* unless you undress that easy assertion,
undoing its petals and laminae, and going in
below all trace of consciousness, into the neuroelectrical
coffer where self-understanding is storaged away,
and then lifting its uttermost molecule out, to study
in its nakedness as it spins
in a clinical light?—the way
we all, in our various individual versions
of this common human urge, go in,
to the string-vibration underlying matter, and
the Appalachia fiddler getting so
(as she puts it) "into my music," sound becomes
a flesh for her to intimately ("in"-timately)
enter, "its thick and its sweetbreads."
Is he cheating on you? *He* says no, and feigns
that he's insulted, but for certainty
you'll need to delicately strip the bark away
and drill, and tweeze, until you can smear a microscope slide
of the pith and can augur the chitterlings
—the way the philosopher can't accept a surface
assumption of truth, but needs to peel back
the fatty sheen of the dermis, soak the cambium layer
into a blow-away foam, and then with pick
and lightbeam helmet, inch by inch begin
spelunking through those splayed-out caverns
under the crust, where gems of cogitation are buried
—the way the diver descends for the pearl,
the miner: in, the archaeologist: in, the therapist: down
the snakier roots of us and in, and in, the way
the long, leg-pretzeled yogi makes
a glowing bathysphere of worldliness and sends it in,
and further in, tinier and heavier and ever in,

the way the man in the opium den is floating forever
toward a horizon positioned in the center of the center
of his head. . . . If we could stand beyond the border
of our species and consider us objectively, it might seem
that our purpose in existing *is* to be a living agency
that balances, or maybe even slows, the universe's
irreversible expansion out, and out . . . and each
of us, a contribution to that task.
My friend John's wife received the news: a "growth,"
a "mass," on her pituitary, marble-sized, mysterious.
And the primary-care physician said: Yes,
we must go in and in. *That couldn't be the final word!*
And the second-opinion physician said: Yes,
my sweet-and-shivering-one,
my fingerprint-and-irisprint-uniqueness,
someone's-dearest, you
who said the prayers at Juliette's grave, who drove
all night from Switzerland with your daughter, you
on this irreplaceable day in your irreplaceable skin
in the scumbled light as it crosses the bay in Corpus Christi,
yes in the shadows, yes in the radiance,
yes we must go in and in.

> *"The lions in his menagerie ate parrots, and he*
> *fed his horses grapes."*
>
> —OF THE EMPEROR ELAGABALUS,
> 218–222 A.D.

And for his human guests, imperial excess straining
all credulity: say a nightingale embalmed in honey
and stuffed in a swan that was stuffed in a tenderized hog
that was levered into a slow-roast ox, the spaces in between
these telescoping boluses made cloggy with impactions
of lamprey, fresh sows' udders, roosters' jellies in pike sauce,
and a veritable scree of goose and pheasant livers
elevated by nightlong immersion in mint.
And they didn't partake of this abstemiously—no,
it drizzled prodigiously down their chins and over
their breasts, it left them lumpishly held to their couches
as if their guts were a fatty magma set on cooling
into the heaviness of stone. Do I understand this? Maybe.
Maybe when I remember my mother refusing even a teaspoon

of the watery broth we offered her—the cancer was
so eminently painful by then, and so obviously
medically unassailable—and when I see her turning
into a project made of fluorescent light and gossamer, ready
to flimmer away on someone's sigh or a nurse's cough.
When I think of Phillip opening his chest and groin
like a cabinet door so we could see how now his once-renowned
gourmet solidity was scarecrow straw the winds of dying
sang through, in their whiny pitch. And when the TV news is
the emaciated—twiggish limbs, and faces all concavity,
and children in these camps who look as if the deathwatch flies
they bear all over them could lift them, in some show
of a ghastly synchronicity, off the earth. And then I comprehend
the urges, or anyway some of the urges, for accumulating

counterweight, despite its often fantastical tallies.
How many separate cheeses and hens compose the single
viscous river of cheeses and hens upended down the gullets
in Rabelais? How many quaffs of sack for Falstaff?
In one Irish poet's twelfth-century lyrical whimsy, his hero
voyages over a "sweet milk sea" in a coracle "built of lard."
"Professional eater" Takeru "The Human Tsunami" Kobayashi
wolfed his way to win the World Hamburger Eating Competition
in 2006, score: 97 downed in eight minutes. Sonya Thomas,
current reigning female champ, is 100 pounds: "I believe
I can handle up to 18 pounds of food and liquid." So we're back
at Elagabalus's palace, all of those post-gluttonizing
snoozers on their silks like sacks of monumental gravity,
unbudgeable . . . just *let* the goons of dissolution come,

the rust, the winnowers, the strafing rain, the tumor . . .
let them try, just let them *try,* to pry these bodies,
these repletions, from their hold on life, or lessen
them a smidgen! And the life of the spirit?—its symbol might
sufficiently be a flame inside a tiny tinwork bird; instead,
we get the Gothic cathedral (Rouen: 495 feet high,
and Chartres: 102 of those magisterial stained glass windows;
individual stones could reach two tons), we get the Buddha statue
as tall as some rocket gantries. Porn star Houston did
500 men in a single afternoon, for one now-legendary movie.
(Even so, that record's been broken.) When the Elector August
of Saxony journeyed to Schwabach for its healing waters
in 1584, it required (evidently) a train of 225 horses
sporting matching caparisons. And yet from this same species-pool

of genes, we've been granted such an example as Gandhi, very
quietly but immovably saying no, and saying no, until
an empire turned away (and he ate . . . what? a couple of bananas

and a modest plate of yoghurt once a day?). Thoreau,
as spare as a slat, saying no. The no that Bartleby says
is small and simple—integrity always is.
And here: the photo of a tipi's framework: through it we
can see the sky and an empty field: the planet saying
no to pavement-fastfoodfranchise-mallorama. *Wabi*
is Japanese for a kind of "beauty" in the diminutive
and the ephemeral, the thing that ego passes by.
Leonard Koren: "The closer things get to nonexistence,
the more exquisite and provocative they become."
An inwardness. An ethereal nod. Anya Solvig left

her life in the Sisters of Saint Mary's; and then left her life
at the Cal Tech Research Labs; and then the Buddhist Center.
What she required didn't require an ohm or an *om*.
She built a room of untreated and unadorned wood, "not
even the size of some walk-in closets in Beverly Hills,"
and here she retreated, to spend her days in meditation
—fueled, the story says, by an evening serving of tea,
and a morning portion of rice, and a single daily chrysanthemum
"for loveliness and focus." Here she retreated;
and she meditated; and day by day she flensed her self
from her bones . . . until, I imagine, she could fly
across the earth, above the room where my mother is saying
at the start of her last day here, no thank you, not
another sip, no crumb, not one more anchoring swallow.

Stopping by Woods on a Snowy Evening

". . . miles to go before I sleep," says Frost,
as if at last, at night,
the eyes shut, and the mind shuts,
and the journey halts. Of course

that's wrong. All day and into dusklight
at this flyway stop, the waterfowl
—as plump as pillows, some of them; and others
small and sleek—have settled, abob

in the wash of the river; and here,
by the hundred, they've tucked their heads
inside a wing: inside that dark
and private sky. The outward flying is done

for now, and the inward flying begins.
All one, to the odometer.

THE WRITING LIFE

Birds

It's hunger and territory
although we choose to call it song.

Rereading Attempts at Poetry
from My Earliest Teenage Years

Frankly it amazes me
—how urgently he talked about death,
this sweet blank flan of a boy

as yet untouched by it
in any way, except for the general knowledge
that lurks in everybody's neural complexitypaths
from birth. How urgently; and sometimes,

even, convincingly. The body with the single
professional gang-commissioned death-hole
where the vein snakes up a temple . . .
or the larger and bloodier butcherwork
the surgeons will make in twenty more years
of his mother's gut . . . he has no knowledge

of these, his world is simple and clement,
and yet his small vocabulary is fuel,
it seems, for death, and almost anything

can spark it to combustion . . . I think
of cartoon animation people running off a cliff:
they'll fall, of course, but first

their innocence and energy will keep them
successfully aerial. The same when he faces
spiritual longing . . . his words are meat

on the altar, his words are knees on the hard-ridged shells
of the oracle floor . . . this boy,
untested by anything more
than a standardly difficult day at school
or a family spat . . . his words, his breaths, like any aspirant's,

ascend in search of the numinous . . .
and I think of the initial zipping trail
of the skipped stone: it will sink,

but not before its moments of magic.
And love!—his assault upon love.
And sex!—yes, somehow, Ess-Ee-Ex,

its etiquettes and its violences
and its stinkflower gravitational pull
and its ice-grip and its swamp of no return
and its beckoning wetlands and its explosions
of small god-pleasures and its nightly tombs
and moon-gates and unwashable chemical force,
its hokey-pokey in the honkytonk,
its musk, its mask, let's face it:

only great ignorance
is up to that task.

Those Early Years

Mine were the usual horrors.
I might say the wrong thing, or my grandma Nettie
might die (she did), I knew that there was poverty
and war, and there were headlines: children
just my age were unearthed in the forest preserve
from shallow graves, and one . . . the entire skin of his back
was flayed off, and was partially tanned (by an amateur)
with eye-holes cut out of its center.

＝＝

But those were anomalies. My parents worked hard,
and loved us to match. Whatever engine drove our lives
through all those early years, it wasn't powered by the dark fuel
of so many others' poems: the iron lung; the iron wind
that scours the barrio; the wrong touch
of a relative's hand, as minimal as a shadow-hand reflected
on the tea, but it leaves such an iron, unscrubbable sediment.
Was I "privileged"? No; but my world was benign.

＝＝

Could I bring it to you? Does light like this get storaged
in a way that makes for visible relay, later? As if
I could be a battery. As if I could be a moon; a solar
holding cell; a granary, replete with the sugars
of photosynthesis locked inside its sheaves. It might be
something like the angels that visited Abraham's tent:
three of them, in beggar's rags and journey-filth. You wouldn't
ever know the light they bore until it flooded out.

＝＝

The northern black and red wood ants normally
build a nest (of spruce or pine needles, for instance)
up to two feet high—although one nest discovered
at Holystone, Northumberland, is five-and-a-half feet tall,
with a dome-like roof, and a south side purposely flattened
to take the sun with the greatest possible surface area.
Worker ants will "sunbathe" there: absorb it, then bring it
deep in to the nest to release that heat for the heaped eggs.

Autobiography: Magic

"I was watching old Superman *reruns from the fifties.*
Every adult male—good guys, bad guys, indoors,
outdoors—always wore one of those hats, like any
father's back then. A daddy hat."

—FRIEND, IN CONVERSATION

Night—and lightning cracked the sky,
a dropped black platter; my father was down
in the basement, "doing the books" for his job
at Metropolitan Life Insurance. Winter—ice
an alabaster mummy case that hardened across the city; he
was "doing the books," was working his attention
to a powder against the emery edge of those figures.
Spring—a breeze was shaking the aspen leaves
like snare drum decoration; he was in the basement,
doggedly making a fit shape of those numbers
in the way a juggler might pattern the air with clubs.
Sometimes on weekends we would drive out to "the country"
and buy fresh eggs or we'd pick a basket of blackberries.
Somebody else would know the terms for the when and how,
the little ring of cloacal feathers and the optimum
insemination temperature for the oviduct—as someone
could expatiate on the globular knobules
holding the berry's sweetness, and say they were "drupes,"
and explain this fruit was kin to the whortleberry
and crowberry—but not us, no, we were tourists
in that world a thirty-minute ride away. What
I knew?—"dinner," "family," "school," "TV."
"Girls," I knew, and a cluster of potent, unutterable
words that grew therefrom. My sister. My comic books.
Nothing exotic. The "neighbors." My "bar mitzvah."
So ordinary. My father never snapped

the leather traces to the hames of a shying sorrel,
never tractored his fields below the whiteface cattle
and dark green pine, the way that Rodney Jones's father
did—or anyway does in Rodney Jones's sweatily sumptuous,
jawful poems. My mother might have thriftily
flattened-out and reused the tinfoil wrap—for there
were months when the rent and the paycheck didn't
exactly see eye-to-eye—but *how* can that detail hold up
as a peer of the sucked-clean pig-neck bone
in the poem from the barrio childhood,
its dance of desperation and pride, its dream of a sharp tortilla
ready to be flung like a discus slicing
the throats of the smug. Or how could our patched-together week
one summer in a mildew-dotted, pungent, tilting cottage
in the Indiana dunes think it should be recalled with the power
of someone's summer in the embassy villa outside of Rome,
those sweetened ices on silver trays and those languors.
"Piedmont," "fescue," a "brindled half-Guernsey"
—Rodney Jones's poems again. I knew the "subway."
Big deal. Once I went downtown to the circus.
It snowed. The spring would bring forth shabby dandelions.
Nothing to grab from which to squeeze the nectar
or blood or sturgeon roe. And even so, *somehow*
a life was germinated there that, after
being cast to the winds and landing, continued along
with the sense of the same astonishments
and degradations as anyone's life—the same move toward
the orchid folds of sex, or the antechambers in which we wait
and wash our feet as preparation for being admitted
into the various halls of heroism, intellectual ardor,
spirit travel: with the mouthfuls of vocabulary
to match. How did it happen . . . out of "dinner,"
"neighbors," "comic books"—such meager seed—I harvested

"teleology," "arthroscopic," "the G-spot," "Zulu,"
"Kalahari," "strontium-90," "botox," "hanky panky,"
"egalitarian," "ruth," "cow pattie," "eucharist,"
"systems theory," "plutonium," "rim job," "Kafkaesque" . . .
it isn't possible, the normal satiated human allotment
of weeping and numinous slivers of hope is simply not possible
out of such zilch. It must be something
like the top hat that the third-rate stage magicians
always seemed to be slyly tapping with a wand
on those television ("TV": remember?) variety shows
of my insular childhood, yes but instead of a fiesta cascade
of scarves or a mini-aviary of doves, "paisano"
came out, and "quark" and "fromage" and "ultraviolet rays"
and instead of the top hat, it was my father's
seemingly empty everyday nowheresville
of a half-price lower-middle-class *circa* 1950s
"men's hat," that—like the Original Cause—gave forth
the entire universe *ex nihilo.* Once, it may have been
Thanksgiving, when the entire extended family was gathered,
some imagined slight evoked a very real tremulous lip
in me, and dampening eyes, and a sullen pout
—I must have been six? seven?—and of course
I was humiliated too by then, and I stomped off
into a corner, into a pitiful snit, and so was ripe
for being coaxed back into the general goodwill
by the right light touch: my uncle Morrie
walked up to me, and sat down in silence,
and gave me A Look, and lifted his fingers showily
to my empty head, and from my ear
he gently extracted two gold coins.

1400

Saps, and the anal grease of an otter, and pig's blood,
and the crushed-up bulbous bodies of those insects
that they'd find so thickly gathered on barnyard excrement
it makes a pulsing rind, and oven soot, and the oil
that forms in a flask of urine and rotting horseflesh,
and the white of an egg, and charcoal, and the secret
watery substance in an egg, and spit-in-charcoal
in a sluggish runnel of gray they mixed
with the harvested scum of a bloated tomato,
and steamed plant marrows beaten to a paste,
and orange clay, and auburn clay, and clay bespangled
with the liquid pearl of fish scales stirred in milt,
and suet, and glue boiled out of a hoof,
and ash, and grape-like clusters of fat grabbed
out of a chicken carcass and dried in the sun
until it became inert and yet still pliable, and lime,
and the pulp of the cherry, and the pulp of the cherry
immersed in egg, and coral in a powder,
and silver flake, and fig, and pollen, and dust, and beeswax,
and an iridescence scraped with infinite care
from the wings of hundreds of tiny flying things,
and salted iridescence, and human milk, and ores,
and gall, and stains expressed from teas, and gobs of squeeze-off
from the nettings of cheese, and rouge, and kohl,
and luster, and oyster, and lees: and so from these
they made their paints: and then
their Gods and their saints.

The Way

The sky is random. Even calling it "sky"
is an attempt to make a meaning, say
a shape, from the humanly visible part
of shapelessness in endlessness. It's what
we do, in some ways it's entirely what
we do—and so the devastating rose

of a galaxy's being born, the fatal lamé
of another's being torn and dying, we frame
in the lenses of our superduper telescopes the way
we would those other completely incomprehensible
fecund and dying subjects at a family picnic.
Making them "subjects." "Rose." "Lamé." The way

our language scissors the enormity to scales
we can tolerate. The way we gild and rubricate
in memory, or edit out selectively.
An infant's gentle snoring, even, apportions
the eternal. When they moved to the boonies,
Dorothy Wordsworth measured their walk

to Crewkerne—then the nearest town—
by pushing a device invented especially
for such a project, a "perambulator": seven miles.
Her brother William pottered at his daffodils poem.
Ten thousand saw I at a glance: by which he meant
too many to count, but could only say it in counting.

3. B. Digital
a. Baginal wall

—*a typo (line 17) from "Outline of Gynecology Examination," a 37-line typed sheet of folded 8 1/2 x 11 paper that, as I was browsing an antique mall, slipped from a 1930s gynecology-obstetrics textbook*

—or, as I said to my undergraduate poetry students,
slipped here into our universe through a portal
in the space-time continuum, out of another world, perhaps
the world they should be writing about
instead of being blinded by the immediacy of their own
impossibly boringly splendid current lovers
and boringly obtuse exes, not to mention
grandma dying, not to mention their totalitarian parents
and ditto their watery angst . . . instead,

consider turning a corner, into this shimmering
cousin dimension, this existence just one silky aspirate
or nanobot or hydrogen solution or presidential election
off from ours . . . "Excuse me, do you know what crime it is?"
"It's yours for No Honey Down!" . . . and make *this*
almost-Earth, this tantalizingly-like-but-not-quite
Wichita, Kansas solidly credible, as a way of honing
(or there it might be moaning . . . see?)
one's writing skills . . . a world that,

though it isn't ours, still speaks for ours
each time her nearness makes his chart beat faster
in a pour of rain, in a power of ruin,
with buttons that require the most persuasive of description
(zirconium-plated; carved of bone) before their inevitable
unbuttoning for a night of making shove . . . just as the war

in that alternaty is asking us to bring it into meaningful
display: a mother lifts her dying infant
out of the fires, and cries her size out. In reporting

on that world, *because* it isn't ours, we need to make it
as durably rock-knockable as ours. If we begin with a man, before
we get to his sex life or his gods, let's not forget how real
the sky should be, and the air at his face, and the weight
of a long day's laboring . . . and then, and *only* then,
think how his weenis is dreaming moonily of the furl and the croissant
and the sargasso and the pudding and the chancel and the rose
and the poblano and the whiplash and the slurp and the concerto and
the hymnal and the sweet magnetic fleece of the nearest bagina.

The Craft Lecture to the Creative Writers
of the Low-Residency Program at Yadda Yadda University, with a Late Assist from Wallace Stevens, Robert Frost, Maxine Kumin, Sir Thomas Browne, and Allusion to the Title of an Early Book of Jorie Graham's

> Neoglyphea neocaledonica—*nicknamed the "Jurassic shrimp"—was known only from 50-million-year-old fossils until a living specimen turned up in [2006].*
>
> —NEW SCIENTIST

The Earth was writing: the Earth had penmanship.
That was my dream. I remember so little of it. I know
that hyenas and, after, pincer-beetles
had made a great clean whiteness, made a bone frond
ten feet long or more, of a giraffe's neck—and by this
I could see that the Earth was practicing cursives.
But the rest of it? . . . a fizzle, another adventure
gathering think-dust on a back shelf
at the lost & found. I tell you,
keep a dream journal. Read, of course: read wide
and deep. Revise. Be open. And keep
a dream journal, and keep it
handy, and keep it a continent of vacant clay
that requires your staked-out cities. It was dawn,
or almost-dawn, it was the hind tit of night.
My father was telling me . . . what? A stick of wisdom
from his pocket package of gum? a joke? a picture of what
it's like to be the new guy at the daily meeting of dead men
and to have to admit you're still addicted
to living? . . . he was telling me . . . but then it was moss,
and then it was a molecular architectural sketch of moss,
and then it was nothing. Keep a dream journal.
Keep it a vast and empty snow

that requires your skitter of tracks: your alphabet. Be rapid
and accurate. Audubon needed to work his birds
immediately onto a page, if the color were going to be true
to the throbbing picante of life, for if he waited . . . the viridian,
the flame-blue, all of the telegraphed dabs of ruby among the saffron tufts
or even the definition under coal-fleck gray,
would drain away with the blood,
the now; so keep a dream journal. Keep it adhesive,
awaiting the touch of a flange of the dream,
a fin, a nylon, a bee of the dream
to innocently nuzzle against the stickiness
and be fastened. Otherwise, every new awaking
is an alzheimer's of the preceding eight hours,
their civilizations' temples and faro palaces get buried
under jungle vine and tundra grass
and the vortex of worry and passion that constitute ongoing life;
and the nightly hundred roanokes,
the thousand amelia earharts . . . only crumbs
a fresh day brushes off into oblivion. This is my shtick
and my stump-speech exhortation to you, delivered in spittle
and neural knotways: keep a dream journal.
Research. Hobnob ["network"] ["shmooze around"].
And keep a dream journal, and keep it
open expectantly at your bedside, in the battle against ephemerality.
Lordy what did *these* notes once suggest as a promise—*Pizza to Priesthood,*
another, *Kowtowing in Cowtown.* Now they may as well be the nodes
and the squirms and the toadstool caps of Easter Island script,
they may as well be the impossible fogbound news
that once—but *really,* it couldn't be, *could* it?—
we walked on the moon. It was the ink of night,
the ebony ceiling of night, and my mother was saying
we can witness the internal undoing
of sixteenth-century oil paintings sometimes on an annual basis

—sometimes even daily, as a face is increasingly veiled
in an ever-finer mesh of subtle chemical degrading; for example,
the face of the infant Christ becomes a bag, a net bag
with a rosebud pout of a closure, that dangles from Mary's arm as she
sits surrounded by shepherds. . . . My *mother*
said that? Well, no. She said that she was dead,
somewhere inside my head, but speaking with the soft eyes
and the wry tilt of a parakeet (from my childhood? *that* one?)
lecturing on the passing of all things earthly, and she told me
to tell you to keep a dream journal, to keep it
for her, so she would have a place to land
after flying all night until sunrise. Save the mothers:
keep a dream journal. Save the ancient sky observatories
from sinking under carpets of creeper and kudzu.
A few of them rise up on their own and wink
in the sun for a moment—Atlantis of course is frequently
coquettish that way—but cities and even dynasties
are no more stable than gleam in an eye; and, as we know,
our own childhoods can't be fully dredged to the surface light
by the derring-do of the surest divers, so even if it's the nearest
wad of bar receipts or burger-blearied napkins, I adjure you
to note there mightily (and accurately), oh I adjure you
to keep a dream journal, I claim you as duly deputized
into that order. And when the curator lifted the jar with the thing
inside that looked like a shrunken, salted
catcher's-mitt-with-a-rat-tail-wrapped-as-elegantly-as-one-
of-Cleopatra's-silver-armlets-around-it . . . that
was a save, a dream journal, so was the jar
with the thing that looked like a star from a child's picture book
(only fallen to earth, so dwindled in size of course, but glorified
in falling, the way that Icarus was, or Satan). These
have been lost: Etruscan; Borneo's Kelabit megalith writing;
and a thousand of others of what were "living tongues"

and had the living day on their muscular, moist, exploratory tips
—their braggadocio: gone, their adulatory paeans to their gods,
and their most sniveling whinings: ditto, their chanties
and lullabyes and war cries and whatever was their oh-oh-oh
of flesh-on-flesh and sexual dew: all, gone.
How many species gone?—a footprint of some dinosaurs could serve
as a hotel wading pool, while others could fit in a plover's egg,
and all of them: gone. A spatula and a glove
are lost, were dropped by the space shuttle crew, and now
the one is almost grabbing hold of the other, forever, up there
in some mystery orbit. "Prosopagnosia": tragic
inability to recognize faces: after a virus
caused an inflammation in her temporal lobe, one mother of four
"can't recognize the faces of her children, her husband,
or even herself." And what I said in 1975 to make Sylvia
weep so?—gone. All of my past lives—gone, the one
in which I slew the enemy host,
the one in which I wore a porkpie hat
and mooched off relatives—gone, the pogroms of time
have made a thinning silt of these. And your innocence?—lost.
(I think I saw it looking like the star in a children's picture book,
but cinders now.) And any reclamation of these
would be a marvel worthy of a dream journal. There are blazons
to be notched on the trail going back. If you see my mother or father
in *your* dreams, write them down—be gentle, as they would be
with you—and then check the identification bands I've cinched
in one of my dreams around their wrists, and give me a call
to tell me how far they've traveled. These have been found:
The earliest dental work from the Americas,
4,500 years old—these teeth the color by now
of supermarket curry, that were ground down so
that they could be mounted with panther or wolf teeth.
Water on Mars. Rivets from the *Titanic*. A face

that was drawn in a cave on calcite 27,000 years ago.
Numerous pieces of chicken from the uterus
of a fifty-year-old woman in Finland (she believed that
"they would grow into a baby"). DNA, farmed from the tooth
of a Neanderthal child discovered in a Belgian cave.
Your high school yearbook. Something under the bed
that doesn't require detailing here, except to point out
water on Mars was far more likely. All of these
instances of conservancy score an *oh wow* on the aura-meter.
Reclaim the forsaken. Work, of course, on your resumé,
on keepin' up, on gettin' down—and think of Viktor Sarianidi:
"No one believed that anyone lived here until I came!";
(*here* being the harsh steppe-desert land of what today
is Turkmenistan) and yes, in fact "Most scholars had thought
that such sophisticated settlements hadn't taken root
in the region until 1,000 years later or more" than Sarianidi proved;
but he had a dream; and he spent thirty years at digs where sometimes
plagues of locusts "filled the trenches faster
than they could be shoveled"; still, he shoveled; in heat
that shovel-whacked straight back at him, and under the threat
of occupying military forces, he chiseled determinedly; and now
indeed we have this further feather in the cap
of our human accomplishments, and from its smallest
artifacts—a silver clothing pin in the shape of a camel
(the point ascending from one of its humps), a three-inch sturgeon
shaped of bronze (with a comical face that could pass
for a parrot's)—we can move up to the scale
of the central citadel and its towers, here in the town of Gonur
from 4,000 years in our past, its orchard canals
with glacier-fed water, its gold and ivory trade routes,
and its elaborate graves complete with wheeled carts
to roll in service along the avenues of the afterlife,
and from these we can move to a world implied beyond

the physical evidence: of theology and metallurgical expertise,
and the agri-lore for lentil and barley, and gender roles,
and the philosophical bullshit-swapping late into the night:
as amazing as water on Mars: another, earlier Earth
inside the earth: another planet really, only
cognate with ours: and the everyday carnelian brooches
and lapus lazuli figures of somebody's version of Irving
and Fannie Goldbarth is entered now in this registry that keeps
it all from going up with the kindling: hoe,
I tell you, the rows of your dream journal. Just the other day I heard
someone say "hooliganism," someone said "prie dieu," they
grabbed these words by the collar just as they were about to fall
off the edge of the map of the recognizable universe. Keep
your own preserve, and keep it pluripotent. Husband
its brawn. What *did* it mean when I dreamed
of a sexy new cop for a TV show, named Rachel Profiling?
—Keep a dream journal. Obviously Proust did
in between the lecture circuit and the interviews: a folio-dimensioned,
moleskin-bound affair with gilt-and-deckled edges.
Dickinson's: straight, square, satin-black; when she was done
for the day with her letters to public relations agencies,
she would add to its pages by the light of a single candle
as alabaster and gently numinous as an Easter lily. Famously,
Bukowski's was a bright pink, with a rainbow appliqué
on top and a teensie heart-shaped lock to keep it private.
Keep it. Daily attend to it. We are as butter
under the summer sun. The only emperor *is*
the emperor of ice cream. Tempus fugit. The woods
are lovely, dark and deep. I tell you *all* of our residency
is low residency. Our ground time here will be brief.
We start with "eros," but add a single final "ion" and
we're crumbling away at the continental rim. I tell you
nothing is more dust than a mountain, no matter

its seemingly imperturbable bulk. Therefore
it cannot be long before we lie down in darkness,
and have our light in ashes. Hail, rust. Hello
to the waves of video blahblahblah erasing history.
When my colleague Don the Shakespeare expert retires
he will not be replaced. *Shakespeare*: not replaced. Now
he will wither at the petal, he will feel the ravening worm
in the very kernel. Last night my childhood knocked
for attention against the inside of my cranium,
a ten-year-old boy and a hazy duo behind him looking
as if he could never grow up to fail or disappoint,
I heard them say that memory is holy, and nothing
—not the son or the Son or the sun overhead itself—is eternal.
Keep a dream journal.

GOD GIVES ADAM AND EVE AN ALPHABET

The Voices

. . . that scheme is too simplistic. It leaves no room for those who read in order to reach heaven, to understand the laws of nature, to improve their manners, or, eventually, to repair their radios.

—ROBERT DARNTON

1.

"My mother worked in condemning." Well whose
doesn't? "No, I mean that *was really her job,*
condemning vacant buildings for the county." And his father:
every night, he would array the day's entire profits
on top of the bed's chenille spread—beginning at the upper left
with hundreds (if any) and working down to singles
at the lower right—then he'd inspect each one in turn
with a giant magnifying lens, like Sherlock Holmes:
"The counterfeiters don't sleep." If *these* exhibit
little closeness to the stories from my childhood,
what measurements of distance are required to describe
the gap that opens up when Nasseet tells his anecdotes?
The time ("I was a fourteen years") he wearied of the monkeys
who would chatter as he napped up on the roof,
"so I buy me the opium ball from a dog-cart man,
and let the monkeys consume of it, and when they sleep
I beat them with a bat." (When we look shocked
by this: "Not dead, no-no. Just bloody.") His sister's
wedding dress, "of many thousand of mirrors, each one
no more bigger a grape." The other sister married
out of the faith: "My father seek to reprimand this man
with a machete." And it's not that these are "foreign"
to the life I know, but that they're *untranslatable.*
In a fable out of one Judaic mystical tradition,

God gives Adam and Eve an alphabet
of seventy-two "original letters." *Seventy-two,*
with the heat of the Lord's first utterance still rising
from their lintels and fiddlehead curls in a steam.
Now when I learn about "the obsession
with braiding dung for display on the tops of manure heaps,"
evidently a common practice
in the middle 1700s in some French villages; when I hear how,
at that same time, in that same place, you could render yourself
invisible by eating the brain of a dead cat,
"if still warm"; or that a woman in Seville was seen
to lift from her prayers in an ecstasy
and float above the pews "until she hovered
at the wooden Christ at least twelve feet above our heads,
attracted to his open, crimson injuries
like a hummingbird to flowers" . . . then I understand

what happened to the other, the missing,
forty-six letters: they created the words
and the ideas of these other lives.
Humility is different here; and horseflies,
and the tiny, sour sex that brings forth horseflies;
and the names that the glazed clay deities bear.
A woman is having a lover carve a silhouette of her
into his skin. . . .
A woman is given angels (or adrenaline) enough to work
her child out of a lion's jaws. . . .
In our world, even the smallest combinations
of their alphabet—a preposition, an acronym—
would take away, like a wave of a wand,
the tongue that tried to say them.

2.

Tonight my wife and I are cryptograms
to one another. All week, really. How long is a night
like that?—how many years? Whatever we say and do
is received at the other end of transmission as scrambled.
Even "happiness"—even something so basic as that.
We discover it's only sounds: it doesn't have a single
consensual definition built into it.
"Happiness." "Trust." "The future."—Sounds.
We may not even share a neuroanatomy.
"Wabi" and "sabi" *(Japanese)* mean things

for which there aren't terms in English: we require paragraphs
to say it (if we'd even *think* to say it, since
to not have the word is often to not have the concept of the word
inside one's cultural assumptions: if the bird
has never existed, neither does its place on the ornithological tree).
This isn't because the Japanese have a higher
word-per-existence ratio, but because
they think in "wabi" and "sabi."
"Yugen." "Awahre." "Shibui." Tonight
my wife and I are reading together, apart;
that is, in separate rooms

of one room. Separate chambers of the heart.
And what we need is to appease the fractious "bongas"
(*Santali*; India) of our spacetime nexus: maybe that
would reestablish "tjotjog" *(Javanese)* for us, and maybe at last
"mokita" (*Kiriwina*; New Guinea) in all of its whispered nuance
would be spoken, and a hope
begin suffusing through the fog. Meanwhile, her book (there)
and my book (here) exist about as far apart as . . . who knows

really what it means to read the way they do the tales
at Bali death rites?—nonstop, "twenty-four hours a day,
for two or three days at a time," these stories
of stories-nesting-inside-of-stories-only-to-flower-
into-further-stories. "Balinese demons cannot turn corners," and so
these tales keep the otherwise susceptibly snatchable soul
of the dead in a guarded space at the core of a narrative maze.
Or who would claim to *really* know the serotonin,
hungers, bedrock gospel truths, cerebral voltages

of being Ralph Waldo Emerson's aunt, Miss Mary Moody Emerson,
who chose to wear a shroud every day as an outer garment,
sometimes riding donkeyback that way through the center
of Concord, Massachusetts?—"August returns! I look at the darkest
events of the winter & spring, I hug them closely"—and "One hour
of visitation to my spirit, and pain & care & the cloud of sightlessness
becomes luminous—the Source remains with the insane!"
She may as well be the custodian of a language
of frozen gas and electrical jump in the skies of some exoterran biology.
Who shares a vocabulary *really* with Hu Ershun,
the farmer in Jiangsu province "addicted to swallowing pebbles,"
who was finally hospitalized "after having eaten,
over a nine-year-period, three tons of stones." If a syllable

of his life collided with one from yours or mine, the resultant
domino-spill might jeopardize the entire physical universe.
The beacons of celestial navigation would tilt and flimmer.
Tonight, however, I would be pleased to understand the laws
that govern just the air of this room,
the dead ends and the trade routes of its linguistics.
The "empyrean"—what? A "look"—translation?
The "fundament." A "laugh." "Reality."
"Happiness." "Trust." "The future."

3.

There are words, "phenomenology" comes to mind,
and "mind" itself, and "noumenon" and "hermeneutics" . . .
we could slug through them all day as if
through wool-thick swathes of swamp mist, and not once
be satisfyingly bit on the leg
by teeth, by actual teeth, from an actual thing
to kick at. —Yes, and that's *our own,* familiar
American English! So it's poor odds
we could ever enter holistically into the distant realms

that give us "mbuki-mvuki" *(Bantu),* "rojong" *(Indonesian),*
"ma'at" (hieroglyphic Egyptian), although we surely have
sore need here of the cosmic *[rightness] [balance] [just existence]*
that the last of these encompasses. But consciousness
remains at home in its matrix of vocabulary, and often
doesn't travel well. When Tony asked the desk clerk
at the Mexican hotel how much a room was,
meaning "quanto," but instead (and this was greeted
with a stiff arm pointing commandingly into the street) asked
if the room could accommodate four. When I
recounted Nasseet's anecdotes in section one; admit it,
don't these come across just quaintly enough to be
a jot distasteful as they work their charm? Although
it's one of Nasseet's other stories that encourages

a faith in comprehension. "At this time I am here
I say one week. I do not speak it, any. Nor do some
bewitch of a lovely lady I meet with at a party
from my boss: she knows not one word of my own home.
Can you guess next?" We can guess next,
we can readily imagine them on that bench in the garden,
moon and booze and wisteria and a spirited goodwill

accruing clear communication. Also "Tatti Valo,
twenty-three, a woman form the Russian Town of Anapa, claims
to be able to speak 120 languages: 'They just came to me
one day in mathematics class ten years ago.'
Allegedly, linguists studying her have identified
16th century English, Chinese, Persian, Egyptian, Mongolian,
Vietnamese, Korean and Swahili." If I'm tempted to believe

in that astounding polylingual olla-podrida, it's because
of this: Whichever's the gene for aptitude
in mechanical matters, it's missing from my family.
I couldn't figure out poot from whiz,
and neither could my father, or his. But Cipriano's
granddad was a maestro from the planet
of Hand-to-Eye Coordination. I would visit there
when I was eight or nine, and watch him mumble
to the lubricated sprockets at the heart of something broken
with an intimacy I'd only see, much later,
was the bed-talk of a lover to the one beloved.
A toaster?—no problem. The television. An oven.
One rumor had him inventing a viable one-man biplane
in his youth, but what I'll never forget

from a quiet evening in 1956 is coming upon him
in the yard as he gave a few quick, finishing tightenings
and an affectionate pat to the back of a large
and many-dialed box of a kind I'd never seen before.
It was a radio, I guessed—and with
such generous bulk, it looked as if it could hold every station
from here to the Poles. And that's

what it did. He turned a button, and heated it up,
and as I watched unnoticed by him
below the efflorescing sky, in the dwindling buzz
of a city street that was already starting to go to sleep
and segue into its thousand dreams, the voices
of the world descended
one at a time and emerged from that grid
like the pearls of a mile-long necklace.

I'm Nobody! Who Are You? Are You Nobody, Too?

—EMILY DICKINSON

1.

She undressed in the candlelight—disclosure
enough to excite me (even given
the intermittency of the vision) and enough
to reveal that right there, in the swan-neck soft of her
between her navel and what a more discreet memoirist
than myself would call her pubis, was an amateur tattoo
—perhaps an inch high, in a clumsy Gothic lettering—
that stated: PEPE'S. I looked for a moment
too long, so she had to say something, and what she said
was candid. "That? Oh, was maybe a year ago.
I gave him naming rights."

2.

The tree, the wind: a fricative relationship.
A sound so shaped that some nights
it's less music and more language.
Words. A few words, anyway. There
have been nights, admit it, when
you've thought you heard your name in the air,
your name being sung, a recognition
that you're a part of the star-resplendent sky
and the musty vapors of earth—they
know who you are, you owe them for this special focus.
Listen: your name; a part
of the wind's acoustical graffiti.

3.

These days it's everywhere. On the highway side
of a stadium: MULTINATIONAL CORPORATION NAME.
On the round of a silo: HUMONGOUS COMPANY NAME.
Mowed into the side of a champion steer: A FEED LOT NAME.
Sown into a field of sorghum: A BEER MANUFACTURER NAME.
In films (and surely music videos) it's sneakier;
we call it "product placement." Soon how much will it cost
to insert your brand in the paragraph of a novel?
(Or does it happen already?) "He lifted his wine and stared
at her with a sullen fixity over the rim"—or $50,000 later
he lifts his Sunnydale Autumn Pinot Noir and stares at her. . . .
How much did it cost for Pepe's insertion? This
is true, it comes to me from my friend who works
in "advancement" (i.e., money-raising) at Blah Blah University:
they were planning a new school library and were actually considering
the selling of naming rights not only to various rooms,
staircases, multimedia collections, and books-by-field,
but also to individual toilets. For the man
or the woman who, as we say, has everything. As you probably know,
a company exists that, for a tidy fee, will register a star
in the name of your choice. It has no standing
in the scientific community, but think of walking
into the night with someone you love
below star Name-of-Someone-You-Love!
It isn't useful: it isn't monogrammed luggage.
But then neither is it a toilet bowl. A few of us
have made our lovers immortal through being granted the right
to officially name a new insect. And I know someone
who contractually must keep the name of a rugby team
shaved into his hair for a calendar year. I know someone
who only agreed to accept a divorce

from his eight-months-pregnant wife if he was granted the right
to name the child. An ugly story. Once,
they probably strolled out into the night like anybody
in love and made gifts of the stars to each other.

4.

And so I find it interesting to consider that
this ostentatious and overprodigious showering
of the world with names is no more in the news than is
their theft. It's common. Identity right now
is as liable to being burgled away as, say, a TV set,
a computer, a purse left overnight on the porch. It happened
to Eva: one day she discovered that "Eva"
had purchased a new sleekola whizbang gewgaw'd
speedmobile and a cruise to the Bahamas.
Standard reaction: felt-like-raped etc.
Evil-doppelganger etc: somebody else, who somehow *isn't*
"else," but technically "me"—the way
a cancer is. Unnerving; and yet
a rightness prevails . . . as if some law of natural proportion
is at work, and as the names (on keychains,
t-shirts, megabuck athletic fields, toe rings, vanity plates)
proliferate, at the same time
some, like overcrowded lemmings,
must be taken away. "And really," Eva said—a day
of one too many mai-tais—"I could almost believe
I deserve this thing." Well, I'll believe it too;
won't you?—there *is* an outlaw other in us,
a me-gone-wrong. In Eva's case
it left one night—it stepped out
with the driver's license adroitly slipped into its garter.

5.

Somebody with your credit card.
Somebody with your social security number.
Somebody with your wife.

Somebody who needs your life more than you do.

6.

2006: We're expert now at obliterating
other people's identity. On the largest scale,
genocide. In Orwell's *1984* the erasure
of who-you-are is a science
—bureaucratic offices exist for its implementation
and perfection, and it goes from paper trails
to an insidious surgical neurofutzing. This exists
in its place on a line that we can follow back in time
to an active theogovernmental attempt in ancient Egypt
to eradicate out of existence—in effect, to retro-abort—
the name of Akh'na-ton, an earlier pharaoh
whose maverick vision included monotheism (and,
by implication, an end to the current priesthood): his cartouche
was chiseled out of walls and obelisks by the thousand: dust,
and dust, and dust again: by now
the powders of those minus signs are reincorporated
into our ongoing fracas. When I met her
six years later, she said, "Allen—wow! Hello!"
I would have corrected her, but . . . for the moment
I'd forgotten hers altogether. That night, in a scumble
of shadow and candlelight no different from the atmosphere
of our first encounter, I kissed her exactly where Pepe had been
before the dermabrasion.

7.

I am nobody.
A red sinking autumn sun
Took my name away.

—RICHARD WRIGHT,
FROM HIS SERIES OF HAIKU

When the moon disappeared it took his face along.

—DAVIS GRUBB,
FOOL'S PARADE

8.

An alloy: name
and subject.
There's a privilege in being allowed to observe
its founding moment,
still with the heat and the damp of creation
flimmering there.
        / Traditionally the Eskimaux woman
in labor, with the community surrounding her, wildly
calls out names. And when the child at last
hears his . . . he comes forth.
        / In a Jewish tradition,
the child can never be named for a living relative:
the soul might leave the elder of the two, to take
new residence. That my parents named me Albert
is a proof my father's father was dead
already by the time of my birth.
        / My wife
—although from long before she was my wife—
was Lora. That didn't work for her,
for a number of reasons, none of them requiring
details here. Let's just say life is thorny;
bruise and disappointment are its nutrients; and sometimes
it can happen that a word is too full of association
to carry into the future. She stopped the car.
She was alone with the day, alone in the car
like a seed in its husk, that the day was pressing down upon,
the sun and the invisible planets, pressing down as if to print
their pattern on this forming thing. "I'm Skyler,"
she said, out loud. And so she is, now: Sky.
From out of the blue.

9.

His parents named him Michael: Mike as a kid, then
Em boy, that was his gang name, then Moloto, that
was when he "was finding his roots," then
Miles Long—maybe you've seen him in *Hard Ramrodders 2?*
There are cases of multiple personality disorder with up
to sixteen separate "lives" in one hive of a brain, and each
its history, its quirks, its name. But then
there's Ellen's mother in the nursing home, who needs
to wake each morning and remember what a "morning" is, remember
who her "me" is in the midst of the aches and indignities.
She looks in the mirror . . . most days,
simply being herself enough
is enough.

10.

And Ellen's mother, Norma, she can remember her way
through dominoes, can talk to her daughter
in loosely narrative structure. There are others
in the halls . . . hey, Dave? hey, Sophie? Sophie?—nothing
answers back. It's like all of those places
that are named now for exactly what's missing:
Thousand Oaks Estates. True Comfort Convalescent Home.

11.

One company buys up naming rights to the race car,
one to the driver's jacket, one to the spandex'd asscheeks
of his pit crew girl (the cameras stick to her
like sprinkled talcum on a baby). "He got her pregnant,
did you hear? They're going to name it Coca-Cola."
That's one story. There are jillions by now. Here's one
that comes today from my friend:

Her hair is cornrowed; he was bald.
Her weight is under a hundred; he reminded everybody
of one of those sci-fi blobs that eats Cincinnati.
She's turned thirty-eight, a black-and-Puerto-Rican mix;
and he was sixty-two and Irish-Hawaiian. You
can imagine, then, the comedy and confusion at first,
when the cops showed up at the ATM machine
as he withdrew the last of the cash, and his
voluminous ID proclaimed him Eva.

"I suppose I'll just have to think of it
as my cottage adventure in cloning."

12

[Charles] Lyell, in his Principles, *introduced additional units known as epochs or series to cover the period since the age of the dinosaurs, among them Pleistocene ("most recent"), Pliocene ("more recent"), Miocene ("moderately recent"), and the rather endearingly vague Oligocene ("but a little recent").*

—BILL BRYSON, ON GEOLOGICAL TIME

And in sixth grade, during an oral report, I announced to the world that dinosaurs existed in the mezzanine. . . .

The pleasures of verbal coinage—of defining the world through language, and of feeling that definition on the tongue, for its first time, almost the vital writhe of a tiny, beating thing—are real; an awareness of the many opportunities for naming seems to be neuropunched into the matrix of us from the get-go. "Rock," some pioneer of the art would have said in one of the proto-languages, and soon her best buddy was "Thrower-of-Rocks." Somebody else, "A-Few-Rocks-Too-Short-of-a-Stonehenge."

Tulips, roses, orchids, strippers, yachts, racehorses, angels strewn throughout their thrones and dominions, superheroes, show dogs, mosses, thick alchemical elixirs, the months of the Mayan calendar, rollercoasters, fish lures, wrestlers, quasars and their cockamamie cousins, all 900 (or 500 or 10,000) names of God, that roll call of Dickens's (Mr. Guppy, Mrs. Jellyby, Uriah Heap). . . . We love the lingual gush of such invention, love to stack them and stroke them and yoke them to our purposes. Champagnes. Colognes. Dot-coms. Clouds. Every visible pock of the full moon's.

Timothy Archibald's *Sex Machines* is a book that surveys your everyday, low-key, often mom-and-pop or guy-at-the-office visionary tinkerers in quest of the perfect homemade mechanized sex toy—usually a version of some dildo attached to a pasta maker, a bicycle frame, an electric kitchen mixer, a reciprocating electric saw, an antique dentist chair. . . . The fascination here is not in how exotic these people are, but how quotidian. Dan and Jan (she's an elementary school teacher) "seem to be the kind of neighbors anyone would want next door." They're also the proud creators (and the namers) of the Monkey Rocker.

The Fucksall. The Gang Bang. Two to Tango. The Ultimate Ride. Fuckzilla.

The Predator. Thrillhammer. One Der Woman. The Erotichine. (Maybe if they're commercially successful, major corporations will pay to see their names inscribed on the vibrating sides of these pounders and plungers.) The Wand. The Explorer. The Mastermate. We love this little "Let there be . . . ," this pour of more and more, it's like those oceanbottom vents that feed the mega-heat of the planet's magma deeps out into the blank slate of the waiting water, and hydrogen and oxygen and a salty, womby stew of microbial possibility start to create—right *there,* right *then*—the specific shapes of nameable existences.

Most of which die immediately; surely they die eventually; or maybe they evolve, to such a fractally far-removed, unrecognizeable extent, the very strangeness of the ongoing life is a death. In any case, names decease. The Mugwumps don't exist any longer, their cause is a scatter of ashes. No one calls for the postilion or uses a hectograph. Bodkins, anyone? And Lily Langtry, whose name was once a beacon . . . Maimonides . . . Yuri Gagarin . . . *Who?* . . . a scatter of ashes. (The inventor of the Holy Fuck says, "Well, I've gone through a lot of name changes recently. I was Raven Solace for a while, but now I'm Ruiin, with two i's.") The names of losing Vice-Presidential candidates? . . . the rumor of the ghost of a scatter of ashes.

We can witness all of this process—the delighted bubbling-ups of nomination, and the following oblivion—if we travel back in time, and go past the Oligocene, and the Miocene, and through the front door of the Pleistocene, to the Inthebeginocene itself: today, with hoopla, Adam is naming the animals.

They parade before him, one kind at a time, while he sits on a grassy promontory, concentrating—not that furrows could ever appear on that perfect and innocent dawntime face, but concentrating none the less. And then, with a thoughtful, doughty breath, the names begin.

And as they begin, the essentialness of the creatures begins as well. Oh sure, they had their individuation already—they had it *technically.* The stegosaur and the pocket shrew were distinguishable from each other. But now, as they're outlined, colored in, hammered to their fastenings by the force of a word—*their* word—an indispensable and unduplicatable character develops. "Rabbit," he says, with a shriek of pleasure, as if he's just got *this* one smack in the bullseye *for sure*—and the rabbitness of this frantic, furry hopper enlivens every angelhair scraggle of lavender capillary backlit by the sun in its swiveling ears.

And then, if there's going to be a bull's-eye . . . "Bull," he says as one enormous pawer of the earth plods past. "Rat." "Tiger." "Saber-toothed tiger." "Goat." In a way, they're like the gypsy's crystal ball: a nothing, a purity, that the future gets read into. With this difference: Adam doesn't merely *see* the future, he *creates* it: "Whale," "Bat," "Flamingo," "Ocelot"—forevermore.

Could anything be more happy and empowering! "Weasel." "Kinkajou." And then the joy, as the day wears on, of further verbal dexterities. "Honey badger." "Howler monkey." "Great tit." "Bird of paradise." The butterflies alone are a language-lover's confectionarium: monarch, purple emperor, tortoiseshell, gatekeeper, chalkhill blue, saint's red, the question mark, the comma, skipper, hop merchant, large heath, northern brown Argus, meadow brown, green-veined white, empassion, azure floater, mountain ringlet. . . . And then the fish! And the beetles!

What *we* know, of course, is how ephemeral all of this is: we know how it looks, this fingersnap of certainty, to the eternity-eyes of the seraphs; or to the steady movement of evolution. For all of his nomenclatural fertility, it isn't given to Adam to think up "history" or "fossil." The duck-billed platypus is doomed: its lovely quintosyllabic moniker won't save it. Nor will all of its seven-hundred-and-fifty-pounds provide a permanence for the saber-toothed tiger: along with other megafauna, it will die out, after several glacial cycles, at the beginning of the Holocene.

And Eve and Adam . . . soon, they'll have a glimmer of what we know. They're going to enter time, and start to be dissolved in its invisible secretions. "Shame" is a word they'll need to coin now. "Pain." (He'll feel it right *there*, below his kidneys— they have "kidneys" now—at the end of a day of back-crunching labor.) "Sorrow." (One morning she'll look in the waters, and see what this does to refeature her face.) "Mortality"—*that's* the kicker! *That's* the vise around the heart!

The Bible is silent on their reaction to Abel's murder, but we can imagine, we can *barely* imagine, the shock of this, the first death ever. Abel *is* a crystal ball, for all of them. Adam only vaguely remembers the carrion birds, the vulture and the buzzard; he hardly paid attention to the maggot; but he must have named them too. Now he knows why. The names of things that they have now! The "mourning veil." The "plow." The "grinding stone."

And yet we can't completely and only regret this event. In the meditative science fiction novel *All Flesh Is Grass* by Clifford Simak, the narrator comes to feel a stirring pity for undying things. He scents "the odor of immortality, the effluvium of that great uncaring which could not afford to care since anything it cared for could only last a day, while it went on into an eternal future toward other things and other lives for which it could not allow itself to care. And this was loneliness, I thought, a never-ending and hopeless loneliness such as the human race would never be called upon to face."

Perhaps "the creature that cares" is as good a name for our species as *Homo sapiens*. Perhaps, on this side of those barred gates that are guarded by the cherubim and the flaming sword, "accomplishment" exists, and "art" and "ambition," *because* we die. Perhaps we weren't fully human until we awoke with an understanding of loss. "Suffering," "beauty," "the blade," "the book," "the monument," "the runnel of tears"—the future for them is an empty dictionary awaiting its filling.

That's a glorious labor, but first they must be brought to this ground zero. It's where we leave them for now, two loinclothed travelers, heading heavily into their lives—"without," as my mother would have said, as if gossiping over two neighbors, "a pot to piss in, or two pennies to their name."

EVERYTHING

How Simile Works

The drizzle-slicked cobblestone alleys
of some city;
             and the brickwork back
of the lumbering Galapagos tortoise
they'd set me astride, at the "petting zoo". . . .

The taste of our squabble still in my mouth
the next day;
             and the brackish puddles sectioning
the street one morning after a storm. . . .

So poetry configures its comparisons.

My wife and I have been arguing; now
I'm telling her a childhood reminiscence,
stroking her back, her naked back that was
the particles in the heart of a star and will be
again, and is hers, and is like nothing
else, and is like the components of everything.

Channeling the Lord

*"She says God talks to her
through the TV."*

—THE *NATIONAL ENQUIRER*

Not surprising—not if the Book and the books are right
about immanence and ubiquity. Then, he would speak to us
through everything. The heart, and the artichoke heart;
the bleeding orange of the sunset as it dawdles
on the laketop, and the mortuary version of that color
in the potted meat as it's tinned in its turn on the can line.
Once there's everything, there is no "bathos." Presupposing
an everything, then "discrepancy" disappears from the dictionary.
The voice in the thickening steam as it issues from a vent
in the dim of the oracle's cave; the voice in the vent,
the bubbling ocean-bottom vent, where ten-foot tube worms extend
and retract and extend in a primal frolic of water so impossibly hot
it would melt a sunken car to dribble. And we needn't be ordained
or on our knees or in a vision-state of shamanic tizzy,
not if "omnipresent" is our key word: then, the voice
of imprecation and measured shipwright details Noah heard,
the voice that gently blew on its waiting materials
to kindle a flame in the brain of Joan of Arc, would speak
with authority through the stately, circumjubilant rings
of Saturn; and no less so through the nipple rings
on sale this week only at The Dundjinn. Fraught. Consoling.
Oblique. Instructional. Through the bush
that revealed the journey's way to Moses, and still it was not consumed;
as well as through the rubbish fire I smote
out of existence just last night in the darkened parking lot
in back of Fat Cat's Snookers & Ale. We needn't be
penitential or mediumistic. Once I heard it
during a visit to my father's hospital bed, a voice

of staticky whisper and prophecy, from the catheter tube
like an alien parasite tentacle extruding
through the artificially widened pee-hole . . . I with bluster,
and he with courage, talking of anything *but*
that monstrous presence; and all the while, the voice
of the universe itself was sermonizing to me
about all of our futures. I don't know you, I don't know
how strong you are or not, and so I won't report the specifics.
Ever since, however, I've been aware of warning and directive
in the least of things—of utterance
apportioned through the units of the world. If there could be
a vocabulary in which "choral" and "totality" were
synonymous. The voice of the cure for, oh let's say
lymphoma, up in the clouds somewhere, the realm of dreams
somewhere; and also the voice of the eggy precipitate that's crusted
to the bottom of the beaker in a failed lab experiment.
The voice that booms through the coliseum gut of the whale;
the voice of a cricket's troubadour legs. Nor can we overlook
—if this is deity we're talking about—the voice
that's also manifest in anything inert.
The voice in a proton. In a polymer. We needn't be
repentant, or fundamentalist, or agog
with the spirit of serpent tongues and myrrh.
We needn't be messianic or scriptural. Once
I heard it in bed, in a woman's body: even silent,
even asleep in afterlove, each inch of her was delegated
to speak of unboundaried pleasure
on behalf of the voice. There is no seeming deaf to that
communication, and not to its calms, and not
to its indictments. And we needn't be washed in the blood of the lamb
or the ape or the triceratops. Proximity
is considerable: the plastic voice
in the dollar ninja action figure might be more persuasive

than the thunderation shaking forth in the stone voice
of Mount Rushmore, of those monumental Buddhas
that could serve as seven-level parking garages with room
in the skull left over to be an astronomical observatory.
We needn't be resurrectionist or apocalyptic or wicca-wise.
The voice in the cracking surface of seventeenth century
Flemish painting. "Phlegmish," a student wrote: mistakenness
is also a proper vehicle for the voice. The voice
inside the smell in the rubber nose
the party clown first whiffs and then forgets,
after rubberbanding it to his face. The voice in a spirochete.
The stars are loud. The emptiness between the stars is loud.
Not that I've ever intended this to be a treatise
in defense of the existence of God; for all I know,
there isn't one, there's just an abstract notion
of a ventriloquist's puppet, fashioned
after ourselves, so that we can speak to ourselves
inarguably, and touch upon the mysteries.
I've heard it at moments of such intense sublimity
of thought and higher purpose, I felt bodiless;
I've heard it in simply resting my head
against my wife, at night, the reddish down upon her
here and there as eloquent as the twenty-first century fibers
of any access screen.
She may be a television, at that.
The light inside, and the coiled tubes.

The Everything Song

She swallows it. And then later she boards a bus.
Above, a vee of geese slants in and out
of light as if it's a semaphore on the move. Below,
a shoal of sardine—the dimes of the ocean. Somewhere
too, three guys in matching overalls shlep
a baby grand piano off a truck
with the pomp and stateliness of pallbearers
at a White House funeral. Somewhere else,
a fly lands on the eyeball
of a girl who was caught in crossfire—lands
and paces and lays its eggs. As, somewhere else,
the aunt is coaching the studious ten-year-old niece
in spelling bee arcana. The clouds are dark,
are lit as if by the blows of a timpani section
—saturnine we'd say, if they were people. Other
clouds are smears of froth. The geese across some clouds:
a thread through swathes of rumpled flannel. Everything
is happening. A man in a sleepy border town
looks out the window and sketches a bus that's idling
while its driver makes a pee stop and the passengers
buy smokes and moons of fried pie:
there's a shabby haze of bus exhaust, and a lopsided pile
of backpacks that partition the sun as if it's a crowd
that needs to be controlled by the assigning of colors.
Everything happens, everything can't *not* happen,
what the universe *is* is everything happening. Here
a woman oversees a particle accelerator,
500 million dollars and two-and-a-half miles wide:
and in it atoms of gold collide at 99.99 percent
the speed of light, at over one trillion degrees of heat
if "heat" is even the word by then, and quarks and gluons
splatter forth, as they did in the formative
first-millionith-of-a-second in the life of the universe

14 billion years ago. And here, another woman is having
the latex matrix peeled off her pussy, that
will be used to make thousands of surrogate sexual entrances
sold under her copyrighted professional porn name,
Mink Coates. *Everything.* The girl who was caught
in crossfire?—now she's only a bag that's emptied
of its elements. Now those elements are being reconstructed
into the bones and the ghosts and the carbon chains
we call the world. This poem: restructured elements
of earlier poems: the geese, the silver flashing of sardine.
A sea urchin. A street urchin. Everything,
the stocks and bonds as well
as the socks and bombs . . . whatever compass the shebáng
contains, the whole of it occurs in every occurrence-unit
time ticks out, in both the apparently random
and the seemingly directed. A bus
arrives. It's been driven through all of these lines
to get here, so a woman reduced to a drug mule
can be led to a sawdust-mounded corner
to shit out the thousands of dollars she swallowed,
even as the aunt says "simultaneity" and
the niece repeats it, thinks for a moment, blushes,
and spells it perfectly. It's dusk. The geese
descend to a river along their traditional flyway,
honking, worn; not our original
geese perhaps—but *some* geese, *somewhere.*

Almanac

Every day something is surfacing out of ozone or whatever
heretofore-unnoticed pixiedust or swill has been
its secrecy: Jesus, taking shape inside a cleft
in the crust of a loaf of five-grain bread—the way
he may have formed originally in the shadows
of the cave mouth after rising back through death to what
was surely, even for his most devoted adherents, sheer
bug-eyed amazement; or also the emperor's honor guard,
who were kept at attention for all of these centuries
in the strict ranks of the earth, and now: exhumed
along with the golden coins and ornamental buckles
that had hovered about them like hummingbirds and moths
in that great stillness. —Just as every day a disappearance
adds itself to the list of the lost: we only see a flash, if that,
of rump get doused in gloom between the trees;
we only hear the girl with the suicide note as she slams the door
of the world behind her—*hard,* to make a statement.
Every day, this happens. Every day somebody earns
his street cred with a knife across a throat (by "street" I also mean
the unforgiving barrens of the pampas, and the wharf at night,
where fucking rights and status are determined
with a brute insensitivity its perpetrators think of
as the swank, balletic arts of mystic warrior-kings);
and every day, because of this, the eyes throughout the community
are kneeling—for this is the function of tears. Every day
I'm writing this poem, a few more lines at a time; and I remember
my father helping me with a botched-up tangle of fish line:
little by little is still the entire thing. Every day, he says this
—in the past; to hear it, you'd almost need the tools
of the archeologists who lifted those buried imperial sentinels
into the light of the twentieth century. Every day, the apricot light
—somewhere; the celadon light—somewhere; the azure light
that doesn't quite know if it lives in the sky

or the ocean; the congested light in the furled heart of the simoom;
the light in the eyelid, with its scraggled beauty
of shot silk; also the light of radioactive decay;
the light a virus comprehends. And every day, a bird comes down
to tuck an inky petal or a small chip of obsidian
behind an ear—to help that person
make the last transition, into the lightless fields of null.
A candle every day, the ululation of howler monkeys
every day, a military drum corps every day—somewhere.
What *am* I saying? What's happening here?
Every day, a simple thing: a tan rag in the muzzle
of a soldier's rifle keeps it free of sand; a single sewn-on button
keeps the wadded old sock toy from slipping
into facelessness. Every day, somewhere,
an eerie majesty: the three deer Rob and Addie saw
one February in northern Montana, somehow frozen overnight
intact and standing inside their perfect jackets
of a thin clear crystal—each, when struck, provided
a different note; or the Siberian lama "seated, still,
in the lotus position," whose body eighty years after death
"is absolutely incorrupt; his hands are completely flexible,
his skin a little leathery but soft, his nails manicured
to a fine-edge finish." Every day, this happens. Every day
for a year I was going to write another line beginning "Every day,"
and yet I canted my ear to the ground and heard my mother
(she was always the impatient one) say *Albie, hurry up,*
we haven't got all day!—that surely was an anthem
of my childhood. What *am* I saying?—this is what
Thoreau says in a famous statement: "Nature
spends her whole genius on the least work." Every day,
on the spongey coves of the lungs; on the ceaseless weave
of the lice through the rained-on pinfeathers; on the intimate way
the habañero pepper licks your body, lips to asshole

—on its inside. Every day, the mildew making its furry continent
on yesterday's pear. Every day, the linoleum. For my father,
I was going to leisurely detail all of this—unstinting.
Every day, the digital fizzles and spurts up there on the read-out screen;
and every day, the set sun on the laketop
like a pour of carnelian tallow. And yet, for my mother I need
to be done. She's down there, I know it,
tapping her foot. I need to finish the job I started.
Ah—but how? The afterthoughts are often
the most delicious! The train of the bridal gown.
The fiery sky-wide scratch behind the comet.
Or the pheasant: it's the tail that's the glory.
And the way, behind the tail, is the trail
where the world begins: a plume of dust,
an endless samba-sway of microparticles, the periodic table
where the feast of the everyday is first served.

In Another

The cancer seeded her; and harvested her; and dined off the best
and tenderest parts; and he meanwhile grieved and he meanwhile
clung for meaning to his work, he was a specialist
in "tissue preservation studies"—mummies—and was lost
in the perceptible down on a child's upper lip that had survived
2,000 years of fen and airlessness, he photographed this,
he chemoanalyzed this, it often floated him as functionally as a safety raft
across the abyss—as elsewhere, meanwhile, someone is remembering
and hammering into forgetfulness and remembering a childhood
so mired in the spew of certain adult uses made of her, that
now her reigning passion is the sculpturing of soap shard
into sleek chaste abstract figurines the catalogues
for shows of hers call "spirit swarm," and these she shapes
and reshapes to an evolving fantasia as intricate as Tolkien's
—as somewhere someone is entering a night of unwise sex,
is arrowing into it like a pearl diver, in the attempt to undo
an earlier night of unwise sex, itself the late replacement
of an even earlier similar night, and so forth in a personal-historical
pattern of nesting-doll recession, every new encounter vivified
the way a leaf is after rain, beaded and somehow deeper
—as somewhere every one of us is heading into the fuel for the day,
the necessary erasure, the place of being subsumed and empowered,
the sweat lodge, or the rinse job, or the high fly over to center field,
whatever it happens to be for a given participant, a given
set of lips at the nipple of something larger than *it* is,
an entrance, a new self, an escape, the barbituate fog,
the tracking of nuclear weapons sales, the mountain dulcimer
and its pristine tunes, the 4-H hog with a First Prize ribbon
that takes the sun on its gleamed-up face as fully as a module
as it's shunted in place for the space station being constructed
in what's almost a ballet at zero gravity, and Della and Earl
and the Jesus van they rattle in from city to city
spreading the Word, with a palliative of a hallelujah

coating their tongues and sometimes running like foxfire over their tongues,
and with the power of the Son of God and His crucified splendor
steering for them, decoding the road map's obdurate arterial possibilities
for them, assuring them every mile, every meal, that Glory's awaiting
around the corner: how would they ever get through this life
if they didn't live in another?

Dial H for "Hero"

Once Picasso told me—on an afternoon of bitter, busy snow
in light so confident, so boastful of its home
in the sun, you'd think we would be sweltering,
and so his observation made sense—that everything
and everyone is as faceted as a cubist day at the beach.
That was the same light Einstein lifted for me
in a lesbian bar—we weren't lesbian, neither of us,
but, after all, we were faceted—and in his hand it appeared
as compact as an apple: indeed, he pared it
using his teeth alone, in a single sinuous spiral
of golden rind, and everybody applauded
as if were the stage show. No, that's wrong, it's points,
not facets, said Seurat, it's all confetti of light (the trouble
with friends of genius—those advance scouts
of the mind [is there a "mind"?] and the spirit [the same]
is vision, like these two, in collision) and then, by way
of exemplification, he dipped his right forefinger daintily
into the ocean—we were at the beach, at dusk—and
when he removed it and lifted it up for my inspection, there
in the center of his fingerprint, like some mythic creature
waiting at the center of the maze, was a single
aglow confetto, acting as a nexus for the swift
oncoming night . . . and when I mentioned this confusion
of at-variance cosmologies to Marie Curie—we were in bed
together (not sexually, I'd like to lay that rumor
to rest), and reading our individual books
by the cool, blue radiation her body cast forth—
she rolled her eyes and said "yes" without listening really,
she was lost in a new collection of poetry by my old friend
David, mesmerized, as if *he* were the hero (and why *not?*
isn't he raising Ben? and didn't he help Patricia ease
her mother through the final gates? and aren't these poems
the result of his dangerous visit to the quicksand

of American conspiracy paranoia?), she was wandering
in the thick of his words, their heft and weft (the way
that certain photographs invite our loopy dawdling
in the up-close weathered texture of a silo's side),
and so I couldn't count on her adjudicating anything,
now how will I decide between the test of faith
and the structures of reason, how will I determine insularity
or empire, yes or arbitrate between a quantum-mechanical state
and the "actual," with my guiding lights themselves
so cattywampus to each other? "And anyway, mostly
it's all lies," said the Baron Munchausen, "what the Buddhists
say is *maya:* illusion. Trust me, I know."
He was sitting across the room from us—I was there,
a local watering hole, with Galileo and Georgia O'Keeffe.
"You're listening to *him?*" and Galileo rose up like a promontory
—in his exacerbation, sloshing the foam
of his Oktoberfest special over our table—and pointed,
apoplectic, at Munchausen with the same finger that once
had pointed through the chill air to the cankered face
of the moon in a time when nobody else would admit
the truth of the sky, "That man is a fiction!"

Alimentary

They'll eat the seat of the tractor, and
its years of ass-sweat seasoning are a plus
but aren't necessary, they'll eat it dry,
they'll snuffle at it and chomp it embalmed
in crankcase oil—the stomach of a pig is like America,
it will take the curry and make it its own,
the kiwi fruit and make it its own, the midnight nosh,
the kielbasa, the borscht, the menudo, the oxtail tang,
the tractor seat, and make it its own,
and the leather fittings and several buttons.
Even if the "leather fittings" are pigskin? Yes,
especially: like is always ready to take like
into its system, marinade a deflated
football in drippings and fling it into the pen
and—*stand back*—see what I mean? Test them:
throw a well-used lycra workout get-up
into the pen, the suckhole, the absorbency, throw a pillow
into the fracas and muck, okay the cereal,
sure, the cereal's a no-brainer, but also the Tupperware
for the cereal; sure, the motorcycle jacket,
but also the zippers, i.e., roughage: what pig worth
its famous piggitude voracity *wouldn't* trample its mate
to get such gleaming silver sinuosity
—the roughage of the pig gods—into its endlessness
of want and chow and evacuate, the stomach
of a pig is like an empire, like a religion,
it will take the pagan yule log
and the cargo plane and the virgin birth
and make it its own, the flood and make it its own,
the little lightning bolts—the roughage
of a pietistic story. Fling your plaster saints
in all of their innocent, whorish paint to the pigs,
stand back, there's only the floury dust of plaster masticated,

or fling your children's potty-bowls of fresh shit
to the pigs and it's the same thing, they're so admirable
in their willingness to transform every anything
into their ongoing vim, their spunk, their splendor,
feed the pigs to the pigs, *stand back,* then feed
the pigs to the earth, the maw, the mother,
the chemical burble, the undo-and-replenish, feed
the earth to the sun, the sun to the void,
the void itself to the wheel of the universe spinning
its want and chow and evacuate, its eternity, feed it
viruses and temple gods and opera
and several buttons, feed it thought,
and me, *stand back,* and feed it your love,
your sinuous wish of love—another little sparkling bit
of roughage for the cosmos.

LOVE AND DEATH ON THE COSMIC ODOMETER: 2

Convergences

A little bun, a little snowdust, just a wee white pillow
of heroin—stolen. From La Reina, she who owns this traffic
completely up to 143rd. Transgression such as that,
somebody needs to die. So One-Eye J, a two-bit mule,
is chosen; he can be found at Sicily Pizza every day
for lunch in the back booth. Eye for an eye, and tooth

＝＝

I was reading (it's what started me thinking
in terms of failed trysts) about the rabbit splat
—a goo of blood and tissue—that they've found
at times on the bodies of planes just back from the air:
although the Smithsonian Institution's Feather Identification Lab
exists to monitor swabs from bird collections,

＝＝

When her clothes came off, in one clean whisk,
that first astounding flash of pale skin,
there, in the dim of the park, was like the eerie beauty
of a tree stripped of its bark; and then she bounded
into a bank of ferns and disappeared as if
she'd dived into the ocean; and her girlfriends

＝＝

for toot. That's really a misthought joke, since "toot" is coke,
not H: but it's La Reina's joke, and every lickass laughs.
The unit assigned to pop this slob is Zeto and Danny Bouquet.
They pack 9-millimeter Glocks, so every hole
will be adequate for death; and on a springtime day
as pretty as a calendar page, at 12:09, they storm the dago restaurant

⇒⇐

frogs and turtles and snakes are also scraped
off planes. A *rabbit* at 1800 feet? They think
that hawks and herons sometimes accidentally drop their prey
straight into the path of a flight.
This gore is nicknamed "snarge," and I can't help
but generalize, so that I've come to use the word for anything

⇒⇐

—they were all around seven years old—delivered a holler
of purest derring-do, a freedom cry, and
followed her into that long green downhill roll
through what was like their secret sea. But she's
a responsible girl, and she'd given her word: by lunchtime, then,
she's home again, a seven-story walkup

⇒⇐

with shots so rapid-fire that they don't seem
discontinuous, but make a single line
of fatality coming from each of the gunmen. And
if anyone gets in the way, too bad. If anyone stumbles
into this pure geometry of theirs, tough luck.
If anyone mars their artistry.

———

or anybody out of place disastrously. When I
was found with Stephanie (who told me she was single)
by her husband . . . that's a comic opera version
of how many times, in the old and confused
and exuberant days of my heart's erratic wanderings,
when I awoke into a wrongness.

———

on the west side over in what they all call Fucktown.
Momma busy again in the back with a man, so
Nella arranges and rearranges her few dolls, then
picks delicately at a scab on her bony knee, then
dawdles over to buy a cheese slice at that place what
sounds like Sesame Street, um . . . *Sicily.*

Where Babies Come From

—that was the book
my parent's generation slyly placed around
the house as if by accident: maybe *it* would do
the embarrassing job. It didn't;
its Euclidean cutaways couldn't have demystified
a handshake. Anyway, even that young, I
understood how bogus was its offered logic: men enter
women; children come forth; they mature to the point
where men enter women. Talk about
"circular reasoning"! What about the thrumming yearn
of god for swan? of dinosaur for dinosaur?
of protein infrastructure for the zing of loose electrolytes
in the origin-water? of element for element
in the irradiant love in the hearts of the stars in the ever-promiseful heavens?

Sometimes I wake, my wife is beside me
generating the small sleep-sounds of keeping on
unbroken through the break between two days.
If I look long enough, of course—until that earliest
preamble of the sun's—she starts to clarify
as a shape, as if the darkness is giving her
back to the world. Soon, she's less a cipher
and more of a plain true thing. And even so,
for a second every now and then, her shape blurs,
like a figure in a watercolor
overdamped—or like the way a drawing
might indicate speed. The same when she
looks at me. That's right: because
we come from somewhere, and we're going somewhere,
at slightly mismatched velocities.

At the Children's Museum, the walkthrough gawkers
see a working thunderstorm in the "weather chamber"
accrue its full malevolence; they slide
on soft toboggan-disks (as "red cells") through
the chutes of a human's cardiovascular system;
they electro-intertext with a robot family.
For the coddled urban especially, there's
a simulated farmstead, where a sim-cow
can be milked, a sim-wheatfield sown
and harvested in seven minutes of sim-time;
plus a room where hen's eggs—real eggs,
shipped daily—are being candled by hand:
rows of tiny astronauts
who have come to Earth from so far.

Not Sumerian

They tried to stop her dying. The son with the money
tried—he shoveled it by the trainload
into her lungs. The daughter made herself
an expert in the illness, to erase it
on its own terms: still it stayed, it grew, and as you know
the eraser soon starts disappearing.
And Jerry, the husband . . . his response was simple
and direct—he would have substituted himself for her,
if he could, on that sheet where her dying was so fiercely present,
they were the ones who looked like ghosts. If he could;
but he couldn't. There wasn't a prayer,
or a pill, or a silver bowl of blood they could offer
from one of their own cut tongues, that slowed
that dark arrival. This might be the story

of Gilgamesh, *the King of Uruk, the builder*
of the ramparts of Uruk, who journeyed far, and far again,
to seek out Utnapishtim whom the gods took to them
after the world's deluge and taught eternal life: and this
might be how Gilgamesh, *the Lord of Kullub, the knower*
of mystery words, alone of all men
entered the mountain Mashu and traveled in it
in the darkness many days, *and still,*
he wept before the gods for Enkidu his brother,
he wore the skins of beasts before them, and despair
was in his face and in his breast, *and still, and still, and ever,*
he and his could not forestall the tomb. This might be
that enormous archetypal proto-quest exactly,

if my head today could hold such ancient grandeur, and
if Jerry's face were not so small and pulverized a thing in the river
of psychic pain that washes through the hospital.
More manageable is a story out of the Little Ice Age,

at its coldest during a period known as the Maunder Minimum,
from 1645 to 1715. In one village
at the foot of Mont Blanc in the French Alps,
there was such great desperation that the Bishop of Geneva
—so the chronicles say—performed a rite of exorcism
to try to halt the advance of a glacier.
I think of them: that noble and silly and tiny man,
with his hand held up like a traffic cop's;
and the ice coming on. The ice coming on
with the force of the planet behind it.

Dignity

They say that the first stage is disbelief; and then
panic and fear, as an entry ramp
to acceptance. From there, one reaches the wish
to undergo the suffering with dignity. There *will* be
other stages, but this is the one that claims him
now, and he rises to meet the occasion as if he's a figure
rendered in a muted palette and upright stance
in a fifteenth-century set-scene, where the air in the room
itself—done in the brassy golds of an armory
or a jeweler to the court, and displaying the fine craquelure
we associate with pedigree—is enough to keep
a person from slumping or frantic gesture; it
cinches one into civility. The two birds on the branch
outside the window are so perfect, they might be mounted
on a bezel. In a world of plague, and soldiers returned
from the war with their legs in a sack for souvenirs,
and a woman so weary she doesn't realize the infant
at her nipple is already dead . . . these birds
and this air and the general hush are not
an antidote, exactly; more an acknowledgment
filtered through will and composure. Overhead, the sun
is a medallion. The clearly perimetered lake in the distance
could be a silversmith's gift. And the angel,
when it arrives, speaks with its breath in a formal
and ornate scroll, bearing the hard announcement.

Too Here

Maybe the gods *do* walk among us, swaggering,
consoling, pitying, lusting for our warmth and inexperience
that must be a kind of sexual veal to them
—whatever, maybe they *are* here, always, invisibly.
Maybe we *do* exist in fields of psychic interconnection,
and the way electromagnetism or gravity is a grain
that patterns space-time, so are waves
—although we'll never be aware of them—of hunch
and luck and telepathy. As for neutrinos:
it isn't maybe. They're showering through this page
and your hand and your heart right now. The moth
beats in a frenzy around the candle flame, as if trying
to whip the light itself into a cream. It can't refuse
the bulb in the bedside lamp, the headlight on the car.
And yet it doesn't even seem to *see* the sun
—the sun is too here for that.

Imperfect Knowledge

1.

The biography where William Carlos Williams's wife is thinking X.

—JUDITH KITCHEN, DEPLORING OVERSUPPOSITION IN
CERTAIN LITERARY BIOGRAPHIES

There are two poems listed in Whitman's original advertisement for Drum-
Taps *that have never been found: "A Soldier Returns, He Will Soon Be
Home" and "As I Envision Surfaces Piercing."*

—SUMMARIZED FROM A TALK BY TED GENOWAYS

The structure of the billowing Portuguese man o'war: I don't know.
And: why isn't it ever enough to be "ceased," why
add the "de-"?: I don't know. Whitman:
given his later fascination with serious (what we would see
as "proto-modern") dance, what might we learn
if only we had a visual record of the movements
in performances he'd watched, and could compare these
to whatever slide and stomp and swirl was his,
between the type-set table and press, in his time
as a printer?: no one knows. (Some experts
could "hazard a guess.") If even *that* eludes us . . .
how to "read" the huge balletic leap of a beast
on the wall of a Paleolithic cave, its clayey umber self
part-trailed like a comet in its wake
[you see? "balletic" . . . "like a comet" . . . "self" . . . and so
we'll never know]: that cave and this one,
where my brain conducts its little introspections,
may not have one flapping bat of thought in common.
The war in Iraq right now: don't tell me that you understand
the deals which enabled and support it,
and that generate a moneysphere around the Earth
of invisible e-wealth Munch or Chagall might have painted

in flight like banshees: you don't. You don't understand it.
Somebody knows the origins of "hurdy-gurdy,"
"skanky," "zounds," the use of "fudge"
to mean a wee prevarication, "23 skidoo"—not me,
no more than I could say why gold is malleable
while some days bullets can bounce off my students' indifference.
And: the type employed by Gutenberg? . . .
was an alloy of tin and lead and once-I-could-tell-you.
(Though really I do know the etymological background of "zounds"
—I fudged.) My aunt Regina died of brain cancer
when she was in her thirties (I was twelve) and there
was a year when words would disappear from her mind
to make room for a brutally scouring wind;
she was a frightening gale force of those erasures by the time
she finally "ceased." The soul—or whatever
you call it, animus, or consciousness—the "soul"
as it rises out of its tenuous mystery mix of people-atoms
and emptiness . . . at what degree
of structural biocomplexity does it originate?
We'll never know, not in *this* century.
An aggregate of atoms we'd call Roquefort cheese
is more dense than a tear—a pebble certainly is—
but where's their leap of wonder and their despair?
For that matter, where in the periodic pile of elements
is ours? Where does it go to, when
our webbing of psychoelectrical linkage disappears?
For that matter, where did the hitchhiker go
—she wore a red bikini and a black eye
and she said her name was Honey but you know that that's
a wee prevarication—after Tony dropped her off
"at that alley, there, by the 'Inn-&-Out'": a shadow
into a shadow: gone. For that matter, what *did* Flossie
—Mrs. William Carlos Williams—think about [and here,

insert your choice of detail: illness, sex, the single arm of the moon
through the kitchen window when he was off on his rounds
and she was alone in Rutherford] in 1912, the year
they married (and, incidentally, *Poetry* was founded
in Chicago by Miss Harriet Monroe)? The most empathetic biographer
doesn't know (and yet might claim the right
to a sort of especially enlightened "insider's assumption": hence
the rabbi/imam/priest on the character of the "soul" *[see above]*).
My wife . . . ? By now you'd think I'd set myself against
herself in bed like kindling
for the low flame of a mutual dream . . . but no,
there are no goggles (of either technology or intimacy) to see through that
impenetrable night terrain, a spouse's skull;
and wherever in her the natives are freely offering
garlands of orchids and hydrangeas to a statue of me / or
toppling it down and dancing around it widdershins
in manic exultation / or simply bartering for the day's
fresh-grown necessities in the marketplace, oblivious
to that iconic figure-of-figures, atheists of it . . .
is Area 51 to my prying. Truly—the country of X.
I passed a touching sample of its roadside signage yesterday,
a long-untended billboard from the '20s or '30s:
[illegible weather-smeared letters] & Son.
Citizens of that country.

2.

. . . Recognizing a person's face requires an intact fusiform cortex, primarily in the right hemisphere. Damage to this area of the brain definitely robs the mind of its powers of facial recognition, a condition we call prosopagnosia. People with this condition . . . cannot distinguish between the faces of even their closest friends and family members.

—SAM HARRIS

I was nineteen and he was twenty-six when he proposed. You know that: it's part of the record. This was on the rebound—he had loved my sister Charlotte at first. It's true, and in the biographies. Still, we made it work. We married in 1912 (it's in this poem: you've read it); we made it work at 9 Ridge Road in Rutherford, we made it work till the day he died in 1963 at the end of eleven years of his debilitation. You know all this, it's anywhere. Bunny, he called me in letters, and Snookie—but usually, as you know, it was Flossie or Floss, until that's who I am now, to you, to myself, and for all of those nights I sat in the kitchen while he was out on his pediatrician rounds

and taking notes for poems on
even toilet paper. I know about
wrote to Kenneth Burke—and
crazy about the women." Pa
yet he loved me, it wasn't a
thing. I had my privacies,
burning coals—and so I gave
alphabetical order in an index
dead as a monger's fish. For me
the coals, are none of your business.

right-at-hand prescription pads and
the women. As late as 1943 he
you can look it up—". . . still
tients. Poetesses. Hoors. And
sham, a person is a convoluted
as stoked inside my head as
him his, that you can find in
that you study in classes as
it leaped—it was alive. The rest,
I didn't like Humbo—Hemingway.

He was a small competitive man. I did like Harry Kemp, a nice man. Marsden Hartley?—he would climb all over you. Our son Paul played at Carnegie Hall: violin: a prodigy. You've read these things, that now and then I've let out from my head; the rest remains, as it should, in an insular space. You'll never know. He wrote of "the spectacle of our lives / with joined hands." "We lived long together / a life filled, / if you will, with flowers." This is all in the books. They were my plums that he ate, so sweet, so cold, and with apology. "Death," he said, "is not the end of it." And: "Listen while I talk on / against time." Sometimes I fell asleep while he talked.

3.

I was on a long flight across the Pacific, staring idly out the window at moonlit ocean,
when it occurred to me with a certain unfathomable forcefulness that I didn't know
the first thing about the only planet I was ever going to live on. . . . I didn't know what
a proton was, or a protein, didn't know a quark from a quasar, didn't know how an
atom was put together.

—BILL BRYSON

The desire to know is so ingrained in Western Society that we take it for granted. For other
cultures, on the other hand—such as Australian aborigines or American Indians—
knowledge is neither a right nor an obligation. . . . No one has the need—or a fortiori
the right—to know everything.

—JEAN CLOTTES AND DAVID LEWIS-WILLIAMS

A dollar is always a single thing; but
sometimes it's ten dimes. And so, the Portuguese man o'war:
a colony. That sounds right—in a way a poem can "sound right."
(Though that doesn't make it true. What Dr. Williams knew
about suffering was a wheelbarrow—when he wrote; and when he doctored,
he'd better have known that ten cc's of [this] [or that] would slow
a racing pain.) Name seven opiates. Seven poems
of Williams's. Quickly: "widdershins,"
"cicerone" (rhymes with baloney, not bone), "ergs,"
"palliasse" (as opposed to "pelisse" or "pellicle"),
"siphonophore." I wasn't sure of "rhizome" today,
and I *really* can't tell you in what dendritic curlicue
of the brain our sensation of guilt is born—or fear,
for that matter, or love. Why Stan and Della are such jerks
is evidently (if my poll at last night's party has any
validity) beyond surmise. Why "20 small, rectangular pits
from an excavated medieval site" in Cornwall, England, are found
to be "lined with swan feathers" . . . there are theories galore, but no
clear winner. "Della?" "Stan?"—invented names; you'll

never know. And even to their "closest friends,"
their reasonings are often as opaque as the night
in a Paleolithic cave—we can knock at that door
until our knuckles are raw, and not be let inside
to where, in the flickering wicklight, all of the beasts on the wall
(and all of the human-animal hybrid creatures) move
as if tattoos on the skin of flexing muscles. ("Penis
representations," maybe even actual "penis sheaths"
for ritual petitioners, is how we first interpreted
the rolls of clay we found at Le Tuc-d'Audoubert, although
we now believe that they were "just" clay-modelers' samples
"used to test plasticity.") The lolled dicks of the boys
after roughhousing: that, and the burls
their nipples become in the October air . . . this scene
is understood *exactly how* in Whitman's consciousness?
We'll never know: both poetry and prose are more forthcoming
on the war ("The neck of the cavalry-man with the bullet
through and through"), on the "gyrating wheel" of eagles' sex-in-flight,
on *anything* . . . except the nitty-gritty of his own erotic needs; the special
guided tour of the memories in his head ("Here, do you know this?
this is cicerone himself" ["My Picture Gallery"]) is silent
on that subject. It's a given (really, how many poems of my generation
evoke it?) that we don't even know what the universe is
mostly made of—what the astromasters call "dark matter."
Well, *I* have a theory: "everything-we-don't-know" *is* that unknown 94%
of the cosmos. (92? 97? Something like that.)
I've *heard* it, too: if a whistle's an emptiness
forced through a zero, I've heard dark matter
keening through the small holes of unknowing, seen it bend close
to my aunt Regina and play on her brain
for its personal kazoo. At the start, it was only an occasional word:
"I'll take the stove to the doctor tomorrow"—"stove"
for "bus." At the end . . . but I was twelve, and they

protected me from the last of that gutted-out thing
in her skull: I could only experience its horrors
second-hand, in the deep—the gulping kind—of weeping
that her-sister-my-mother served as a small
ventriloquist's dummy for; and in the way our failed hopes
went down the row of one purported cancer-curer
after another. (We will never cure it: not, anyway,
in this century.) And *you* can hear that wind,
as well—its shrill of teasing absences—and you don't require so difficult
an instrument as a gas-ring formed on Saturn or the circle
of buzzards above a death; no, simply set your ear to a lost
hair scrunchy on the sidewalk, and out of it
spirals the suckhole howling of those angels
who see to our ignorance—the angels of withholding
and the angels with the blindfolds in their hands, a host enough
of the otherworldly to make even televangelists doubt
their pulpit-thump certainties. A wind like that
begins in the caves of our first shit-frightened puzzlements
(*the lightning powers—who* are *they? the bear, the kneel-in-the-dark,*
the sex, the death, the hunger powers—who are *they?*),
and listen: we can hear it skreeking still, these shaky millennia later,
through the chinks in the face of Ramses the Second
in Shelley's "Ozymandias." (Shelley? "Shelley" *who?* According to
today's pop quiz, my students don't know.) And listen: those blanks
intentionally used to structure some of the lines
by . . . whatshername? Duh. Graham. Something Graham.
Well, no single human being can know *everything*:
we're each a partite contribution.
Otherwise the universe would only require one of us at a time.
Now: when did the Suez Canal first open,
what (presuming electrical charge is involved)
is the total wattage of our average dream, and who

are you in your spouse's subconscious? All together,
we might know—like a colony,
like a Portuguese man o'war
(*i.e.*, a siphonophore).

4.

A Semblance of His Lost Work Appears, with the Radio News in the Background and Then an Oldie from Bette Midler

A soldier returns, he will soon be home,
Out of the haze of cannon and the smoke of a city sunder'd,
He returns, he will soon be embrac'd,
He, who possesses but one arm now—a mother's arms encircle him,
He is incomplete, but he was not left cold upon the war-ground,
He is not of that 600,000 *and 43 killed today by insurgents*
including a group of 17 children as carrion,
They are sacrific'd as surely as if on altars,
Those who could not crawl away *had gathered when U.S. troops*
were distributing candy nor is he the soldier,
A youth, or to be frank now, only a boy, a Drummer,
I spong'd the sick-damp from his brow, he was perhaps fifteen,
And merest atoms of manliness coating his cheek as yet,
And in his wound in his side the bone was apparent,
And in the bone a mass of the gore of life was apparent,
In the candle's light this blinked as if a boy was hiding inside the boy,
And I watch'd through the night as that glimmer fail'd,
And lo! at the morn it was gone. *We lost our baby in the Korean War,*
I still don't know what for;
Don't matter any more is none of these, is only himself,
I see him approaching his old home, over a hill,
I dream him daily, he is with me
(Always, even unto hauntingness),
As I think of a people rended,
As I envision surfaces piercing.

There are always limits on what we can know about ourselves, about others of our kind, and certainly about those of another species.

—KAY REDFIELD JAMISON

I could study this crude / Drawing for hours and still / Not figure out how it's done.

—GREGORY ORR

And then Larry drops her off. And then John.
Dashawn. Ed. Hoosan. Timothy. "Have you got
any money for cigarettes?" She's Silk.
Kreem. Amber. On one corner, Bree. And Honey: we know
that if we know anything. Then: gone. Reclaimed as theirs
by the enigmas of the night, with only a half-used packet
of rolling papers left behind on the passenger seat, or a lighter,
or a hair scrunchy—the Ocean of X is always busy depositing these
small uncontexted huh?-parts on the sands.
A used and wadded-up [huh?]. A *10% Off* coupon, good
at [Huh?] & Son. A headline, BLAHBLAHBLAH IRAQ,
as it floats in its daily [huh?], unconnected to blood,
untethered to oil, no equating it to this five-year-old
in a motionless heap at the market, under a circle of flies
that whines in a language older even than human death.
"My name is Ozy*[illegible weather-smeared letters]*. "Oh yeah?
My name is Albert Go[the statue topples, and my wife wakes up
with quick scared breathing], *(scared sounds),* Why what was it,
(leave me alone) / (come hold me), I don't know. Oh we,
oh we, oh we don't know. <(to be read as a vapid singsong). And
sometimes when we *do* know . . . we still don't know, as when I looked up
from the page and laughed at my nanosnap of idiocy: *penology*
is *not* the study of writing instruments. Sinuous wind
through a hollow tree, a particle accelerator, a pinhole.

Even so, at times the touch of a blessing attends to such
enforced obscurity; there *are* things we *don't want* to know,
and shouldn't know, and *really* shouldn't tiptoe through the bedroom dark
without disturbing him (or her) and sneakily open the bottom drawer
to discover. The brain itself is built to be
a weeder-outer; this is *why* it possesses the necessary ability
to generalize, to free us from accepting every new
encyclopedic crumb. And anyway, we do know more
with every generation; if the human genome can, with viability,
be likened (as it often is, in journals for the interested
lay reader) to the keys of a piano . . . now we're done with fumbling
"Chopsticks" and the full command of "Rhapsody in Blue"
is at our fingertips. We do know more—and more
is always declaring its immanence, out of the inky void. For
example: the asteroid Albert, first recorded in 1911
and then, due to miscalculation, lost—a true
two-mile-diameter hole in our understanding—was found
after 89 years, when astronomer Gareth Williams was noodling around
with a run of recent observations, stopped dead-middle of things,
and said (and here's a quote to echo across the annals of science),
"That looks like Albert." "Zounds!"
is from "God's wounds" (a euphemism, masked
as a contraction); let me add the coinage "zosions" here,
"Regina's erosions"—every day a little less cohesion,
every day another rupture in her neural dictionary.
And the type employed by Gutenberg? . . . a metallic alloy
of tin and lead and antimony (rhymes with "cicerone,"
"a guide who conducts sightseers"). Our last sight here
is of a man who is indeed in the process of setting type.
Years later he'll even compose (and so I use the verb
in both senses) a poem of praise he'll title "A Font of Type,"
the various faces ("nonpareil,
brevier, bourgeois, long primer") presented as every

human possibility ("wrath, argument, or praise,
or comic leer, or prayer devout") in a patient simmering: "slumbering,"
as he puts it, "within the pallid slivers"—gibberish, awaiting
its great synthesis in words. It's 1848.
We find his roisterer's slouch hat tossed into a corner,
and his sleeves rolled up, his apron with its smudges
like medallions. And now he readies the scarred composing stick.
And now he swivels between the two case boxes (upper-, lower-).
What he's called "the pleasing mystery
of the different letters." It's afternoon, and light
the shade of a pekoe tea is entering the shop,
an azure and aqueous light, a light the gray of butchers' bones
—an American light, abubble, and composite.
He'll work his trade at these: the *Long Island Star,*
the *Long Island Patriot, The Freeman, The New World,*
The Statesman, the *Evening Tattler,* the *Brooklyn Evening Star,*
the *Brooklyn Evening Eagle, The Aurora*: a song,
those names—a rhapsody in black,
a resistant printer's ink. He's heard America singing,
and he'll sing as well—he'll sing of the body electric.
Pirouetting now, about the shop: a heavy, laboring pirouette
as balletic as the living champagne flute
we call a jellyfish. Even as he sets
a final sentence for the day, he cocks an ear against the air
. . . a music . . . glorious, though imperfect . . .
sets, and cocks, and whirls,
incipiently moving—we might say grooving
to the song of [him]self.

TABOÓ, COUNTERFEITING, THEFT, OBLITERATION, AND OTHER ERRANCIES

> *"... a museum, of sorts, for errors."*
> —NICOLS FOX, *AGAINST THE MACHINE*

1.

The docent is late (she took a wrong turn
off the interstate) and in the wrong gallery.
Amy—that's her name. The tag she grabbed on the run,
from out of the office's tags box,
says Lateesha. "This way, please"—just now
she's leading them to the newly renovated
Hall of Celebrity What-Were-They-*Thinking?* (i.e.,
Britney Spears's kwikee Vegas marriage that lasted fifty-five hours).
Somehow, though, they wind up in the crowded Rotunda
of Scientific Fallacies, at the glass case
where a homunculus is unrolled under the pitiless wattage,
adhesive and fishy, looking as raw
as an infant's leg in the burn ward. Once
we grew from this: yes, all of us. We grew from this
below the blemishless sun
as it circled around the Earth.

2.

Alexander Hamilton: "Why yes, of course I accept
this invitation to duel with Mr. Aaron Burr"
—*what* was he thinking? Based on nothing more
than pen-pal correspondence for four-and-a-half years,
Tracy Cope, a British citizen, flew to Asheville, North Carolina,
and there "she wed James Lewis Morgan at the prison
where he's on death row for the murder of a woman
he stabbed forty-eight times with a broken malt liquor bottle";
now the newlyweds "will get to see each other
for ninety minutes a week, with a wall of glass between them."
What is she *thinking?* Science
thrives on error—that's the way it arrives
at the shape of the truth—and evidently so
do all of us, out battling through the overmuch, the undertow,
the hurlyburlyesque of human lives.
To evolution, the dodo wasn't "a failed experiment";
it simply was its dodo self for its dodo while
—maybe that can help us bring a sprinkling of affection
to our dead-end one-night stands and crashed investments.
So there *should* be this museum that displays
the fall of hasty, failed paint-and-plaster chemistry
that's flaked for all these centuries from the very air
in the room of da Vinci's *Last Supper*; or the Zip-a-Talk,
which intended to carry "electrically-conducted conversation"
through "the universal etherium." "And here,"
our docent says, in sadness tempered by a year
of Monday-through-Friday familiarity, "is the bullet,"
or more accurately the .54 caliber ball—one ounce
of ugly intention—that, a little after 7:00 AM on July 11, 1804,
on a narrow ledge about twenty feet over the Hudson
near Weehawken, New Jersey, exited the smoothbore pistol
aimed by Aaron Burr—who was then vice-president

of the United States—and struck Alexander Hamilton
on the right side, making a two-inch hole above his hip,
fracturing his rib cage, ricocheting off the rib, up
through the liver and the diaphragm, and then
splintering the second lumbar vertebra and,
thirty-three hours later, resulting in Hamilton's death.
Yes, here it is: on a sky-blue velveteen pillow
edged in amber frogging: something like the dot
some archeologist might retrieve from over the *i*
in "bad idea."

3.

Bad ideas.

According to Gordon S. Wood's research, "Hamilton,
acutely conscious of his honor and sensitive to every slight,
was the principal in eleven affairs of honor
during his lifetime." This is one of the factoids
Amy knows, who takes her docent responsibilities
seriously, and some nights—for a unit
of comparison—takes them home.
Example: Marrying Ed was a bad idea,
the dickbrain rat. The baby was an accident.
The divorce was a good idea—of course—but sloppily done,
and to her financial disservice. Now they only speak
to each other through lawyers: less effective, even,
than futzing around with the electro-coiled helmets
and Frankenstein laboratory attachments of the Zip-a-Talk.
But there are bad ideas, she thinks—"innocent bad ideas,"
in that they only harm the consensual—and *baaad* ideas:
George W. Bush's invasion of Iraq will one day merit
a place in the Hall of Mendacious Ineptitude in ways
her own small-term miscalculations of the heart
and the crotch will not. And the baby,
the "accident": it turns out that her daughter is
what saves her from self-pity and abandon: like tonight:
when she retrieves her from the sitter,
there's a burble-up of formula that's dried now
to a lazy sea foam over her chin, and everything else
no matter how global and dire takes its place
in the shadow of this wonder. One exhibit at the museum
is those blind albino cave fish we've discovered
in various similar sunless eco-niches scattered about the planet;
"errors"—if everyday salmon and trout
are "correct"—and yet you *know* they turn

and dart and home like compass needles,
with a bioexpertise exactly appropriate
to their sightless lives. That's *her!*—somehow,
against the grain of "should," she's made her life work.
Other women (as she warms up a bottle of formula,
she warms up to her topic) shouldn't be *allowed* to have children.
The radio story this morning . . . someone
held her baby's leg to a grill of live embers
"to teach it a lesson"—which it must be contemplating
in the burn ward now, the leg a sticky length
of pain, and the equal pain of the lesson
more invisibly relegated to a sealed mouth
in the back of the brain, for the rest of its life.
That woman.
What she thinking?

4.

The architectural plan was gorgeous.
And the shell as it was constructed at the top of the hill
(for they wanted their library complex to be "the crown
of the university neighborhood") was correspondingly
gorgeous. Even, maybe especially, the opening ribbon-cutting
champagne celebration that afternoon: sublime.
And the following morning, rainy, slippery, revealed
that the entire building had slid down to the base of the hill,
the weight of the books they had just placed on the shelving
. . . not accounted for.

On a blunder scale of 1 to 10 (as hairstyles go)
the mullet was surely a 7. We can see
that now. And yet those people got sex
and held political office and played the mandolin
and spoke with God and collected ceramic thimbles
like anyone else. It's here,
a representative one, in Case 11-C:
a sort of roadkill-looking raccoony item,
limp and weather-streaked and formerly blowdried.
Here in 14-A: this lumpy, dull-gray platter is a model
of the flat Earth. It's a silent panegyric
to a (literally) outmoded world. And next to it
in 14-B, and looking like its long-lost twin: a model
in clay of astronomer Fred Hoyle's theory
of steady-state expansion, that's since lost out
to the rival Big Bang vision. (He was a brilliant seer,
although his obituary in *Nature* said
that he "put his name to much rubbish.") Over in 69-South,
a perfect one: a stupid night;
of stupid love; that somebody captured on Betamax.

And one day maybe the possibilities
we so eagerly spin and luster and jam
our hopes inside of will be on display:
a translucent and blobby mock-up of memes
("They thought there were *memes?*"), a long
list of "political correctness" on a sanitized scoll,
and the bowl of plastic spaghetti above its burnished plaque,
String Theory. And even so,
we muddle along, as they muddled along (and begat,
and begat, until we were here), religiously
and scientifically lifting their pouches of lilac and chamomile
to their noses to ward off the Plague, and ditto
pendants of garlic for vampires, ditto woven eyes
to counter the "evil eye" of the Jews, while overhead
the planets of the Ptolemaic sky revolved and oversaw
the machinations and lice of kings,
the sputtering joys and monumental sufferings and lice of the rabble,
as if their solar system had been Banged out from the mind of God
from zero to forever.

Ed was like those library shelves—a thought she has
each time she leads a group past the exhibit.
An unforeseen and impossible weight. But some days
an insouciant sense of rightness claims her nonetheless.
Tonight, after tucking her daughter to sleep,
it's with a wry look that our Amy surveys
her face in the bathroom mirror and tells it,
"Way to go, Lateesha."

5.

She was thinking she didn't have enough money.
Thinking she didn't have enough sex. Thinking
she was fat or skinny or out of weed and thinking
how she loved the baby, the little-her, and hated
the baby, the drain, the burden, the never-ever-ending,
and she wanted it to smile like anybody would,
and she wanted it to shut up, and the phone kept ringing,
and she thought this guy she knew was interested
or something, and the rent, and the pain, and the baby's cry,
and it wouldn't stop, and it needed to learn
what's right from wrong, and the phone, and the noise,
and its leg, and the embers.
That's what she was thinking.

6.

It may be a mistake
to bring myself into the text of the poem at its last.
I'll chance that. We'd be paralyzed
if every possible fumble required days
of gingerly hesitation. It's a mistake
to believe that anything's "solid"; really matter
—us, a pebble, a Happy Meal toy, a stadium—is emptiness
in emptiness, a field of unthinkable quark existence.
A stone: an emptiness. A Rembrandt portrait: an emptiness.
And even so, in bed tonight beside my wife,
I stroke her back as if it's really there,
as if the glide of hand along the roll of skin
were really there and really mattered.
I'm wrong, I know. And yet I go on stroking anyway.
As if the pleasure outweighed the void.
As if we care.
As if there were a place where even I belonged.

Swallow

Sometimes the dominatrix simply squats above
the subservient mouth, and feeds it
like a mother bird. At other times (in other moods)
a sense of courtly ritual is called for, and
her seat-on-hollow-box is wheeled out,
so something formal and geometric is made
of the hovering, pungent gift and its hungry recipient.
He knows all about this taboo need—has never,
himself, partaken; but he knows. He's sniffed its edges
and he's spoken its argot. He knows
where float-heads go for their opium fix, and how
it's prepped, and what show they allow
the rope-and-leather girls from next door to perform
(for uptown clientele) on their waxy, abandoned bodies
while their dream-life is adrift. He's seen enough of this
to have its stink in the folds of his clothes
on the following day, and he knows what sipping use is made
of the cannulas and tampons at those ceremonial gatherings
of the Goth arm of the lycanthropes—their shared sense of community
and their preference for heraldic tableaux.
If it's nocturnal, he knows.
If it's a dark, dark flame, he's beat his wings about it
to the point where just the first few fragrant molecules of singe
attest to the fact that smutch is here in the lining
of everything. If it's sediment, he'll want to take
his one appraising lick—and whether we voted him there
or not, he's our ambassador: our witness.
I was visiting him; we walked around the hill land
to the north of the city. When he was a child
his mother would affectionately call him "little dirty bird."
If only he were. He's ashamed: he has neither the courage
nor the weakness to become that thing, in any
all-defining way. He's something worse:

and he pointed, in demonstration: there, above the pond,
a swallow was sleeking down,
as they do, to drink while on the wing. You can see it
fifty times a day around here: the angling-in and quickening
approach of that serrated shape,
and its barely zipping a beak-trail
over the surface of the water. "See?
A skimmer." He said it disgustedly,
despite the lustrous beauty. And, true, it doesn't ever go
under; only low, and lower.

Evan's Mother's Urine

In one way, it's the opposite
of a river stone: it only gleams

outside of its source.
He looks at the bag that fills,

this first day after her bladder surgery,
with its waxing amber. Honey,

from a hundred-and-fifty pounds of body
and into this three-ounce hive.

He thinks it's lovely
in a certain light of day

and mind. When he was a child, he kept
a stone from the nearby river

in his room, and sometimes set it
under his tongue, for the spit

to reenliven its depth of shine.
That taste! . . . he thought of it then

as taboo, and it would call to him
at night from the drawer where he stored it

curatorially—would goad him
with the promise of a flavor

from the fluid, matrix quick of the planet.
Lovely: as a mandrill's face is lovely,

but no bride is going to walk the aisle
carrying one instead of a bouquet:

there are parameters and edicts
even for beauty—perhaps especially for beauty.

One night at the start of the second week
of her confinement, he was in the kitchen,

over the trash, holding her latest
golden-toned achievement in its plastic sack,

remembering—*imagining* remembering—
their halcyon collusion, in the days

when they were the halves of a system
mediated umbilically . . . and suddenly in one

smooth move he dipped a finger, up to its knuckle,
into that liquid and licked it off . . .

a small connect, an emdash
to the quaggy interior text of her.

"In homage," as he put it to me.
I heard this from his own lips.

Drongo

Not even when she was diagnosed; or when they stilled her sobbing
with the anesthesia, then wheeled her in; or when she was released,
without her bladder but, instead, a bag
that turned this intimate alchemizing inside-out . . . not even
then could Evan cry for his mother, although the sorrow
was honestly in him, in his head, in a lump up there
like a portion of salt-pork that a sailor might gnaw:
it was private, it wanted to stay in the dark and fester.
When he finally did cry, a grade-Z cheese-o-rama movie did it:
lushly weepy background music, and a noble band
of refugees attempting to clamber doggedly over a mountain
(and against the oath of a dragon-riding sorcerer of the kind
whose faux-Shakespearian rantings dominate such films).
It was, he told me, as the few remaining members of that troop

descended safely to the mountain's farther side, and the sun
and the synthesized orchestral overflowing combined into one
sublingual emotional cue the size of the entire theater (after all,
a movie screen is up to 80% of our visual field) that he yielded
to this sanction, and he poured out woe, enormous unpluggable
torrents of woe, as if he were an industry that was hired
to produce enough of surplus tears for export
to the woe-impoverished rest of the world. "I sat there,"
he said, "until an usher led me outside like a five-year-old."
This is why heroic grief is commemorated in gods with the bodies
of stars and cosmic vacuum, in a sky we've made our storyboard:
because we also burn, we struggle mightily with the void,
and with the glory of light and with its disappearance: we need
those stars, the way we need the hypershlock of Hollywood:

to give our hearts their accurate, correlative expression. It
was true, his mother *is* trying to climb the world's
most perilous mountain—only inside herself; and there
she fights her dragon. Its great hunger: for her bladder
only seemed to tease that appetite. And true, too, when the sorcerer
—the dark force of that movie—toppled down a ravine, to the pyrotechnic
special effects of his death, it made a moment
when each member of the audience felt emptied of whatever
individual misfortune tortured him or her: symbolically,
what plagued them had been driven from the village;
they were left clean. It's so good to have a Jew to blame, to whip
into the borderlands; a woman to mark with a scarlet A;
a messiah to die for your sins; a spry factotum to leap and take
the bullet intended to splatter you chest. A lovely version

========

of this is current in the markets of Hyderabad, in India:
the locals believe they can buy "a black drongo,
a crow-like bird," and whisper their problems into its ear,
and release it . . . as it flies away, the trouble flies away.
A rougher version is in Orwell's *1984:* the state knows
it can only break the will of Winston Smith if he'll betray the one
he loves: and when he's threatened with a cage of rats
attached to his face, indeed he screams out "Do it to Julia!"
She becomes his drongo. Once, I visited the hospital
with Evan. In the room across the hall, I saw a woman
—she way maybe fifty, black, and on her knees
beside the bed that held her father—whisper loud enough
for me to hear, "Lord, let some white man die instead." And no,
it wasn't pretty; but then neither was her circumstance.

========

A 15-year-old Indian girl called Savitri was admitted to hospital suffering from tiny stones that emerged from the corners of her eyes. Said Dr. Ragho Saran, "Stones are formed due to the high level of calcium in the body. But they are usually found in the gall bladder and kidney. This is the first time I have ever heard of stones coming out of the eyes."

—ARRANGED FROM *THE FORTEAN TIMES*

If I thought true enough, could every one arrive in the shape
of its specific heartache?—a house with a hole in the middle;
a teething ring; a knife on the bed. . . . And feel free
to put in an order for yours. Because I need to believe
I suffer this with purpose: I need assurance that the ocean
of our misery is channeled as a hardness
through these two pink gates, the better
to be eloquent. For you. Because, admit it, there have been days
when the stone of contempt was heavy in you—and yet
you couldn't say it; the stone of the fear of death was a blockage
inside—and yet you had no public voice. The stones,
the mountain of stones, the filibustering stones, but not
one outward sign. Well . . . here I am. And here they are:
compacted: aphoristic.

Danielle Suite

"This is one of our First Folios. Of the thirty-seven plays, about half appear here for the first time. There are no surviving [manuscripts]. If it weren't for this book, we would not have these plays."

—RICHARD KUHTRA, OF THE FOLGER SHAKESPEARE LIBRARY, IN
WARMLY INSCRIBED BY LAWRENCE AND NANCY GOLDSTONE

1.

The *real* story is: that they
were making guttersqualling love (a fake,
asexual version for the cops: that they were sleeping) when a deft,
tiptoeing enterer raided the first-floor study: there went
his computer. And, without a backup disc, there went
a long three years of labor toward his dissertation on "Intergenerational Lines
of Association in *Genesis*." You'd think his topic would have taught him

better: *The Antiquities of the Jews** assures us Eve and Adam
had a third son, Seth, the august head of a school of astronomers
who tried to crack the star-code and the language of the changing moon,
who wrote their deepest knowledge on a pillar of brick
and, "should this pillar of brick come to destruction, also
on a pillar of stone" erected "far in the land of Siriad."
A comfort, that the stone was there.

The people might suffer affliction of sundering flood
or of the sun without surcease—and yet the stone was there.
Affliction of festering boils, of the death of the herds,
of the lash and the spear of foreign hordes—the stone was there
in Siriad, inviolable. And let the rivers dry,
or let the minions of the The Evil One Himself descend
—but the stone, the pillar of stone, was there.

---

* Flavius Josephus, A.D. 37–100

2.

It made a minor irony that forced itself on Duane and Annie
only after the cops shrugged off any viable hope
and bid our heroes a brusque adieu. Another minor irony:
they *were* devout adherents of backup capability
—only, not on disc. They wanted a child,
a them in reserve. They flew "together" to a party in San Francisco
but on separate planes: in case. That night—the burglary night—
they were into their raw, rambunctious sex
below a vintage Edo period print of "Ukiyo-e" erotica,
imitating its ritual poses: there she was,
stretched into an arch, a decorated cloth
bit in her teeth as if to stamp it for the ages
with her passion, and her toes intensely rounded
like ten shrimp in the curl of her coming.

3.

The honey is sweet, but the stingers of the bees . . . !
This symbolizes her breast: a hive

of satisfaction, and its many little stabs.
She's going to make her songs
(about her loves and their consequences)
eternal—this poet, this Sappho. The wind
that lifts her hair and the hem of her gown,
and lifts our aspirations when it wants
and, when it wants, as soon abandons them . . .
the wind is eternal. The waters are eternal. And the pliant song
she creates as a gift to the wind and the waters? . . . eternal!
Yes—she feels it *that deeply!* And yet,
of course, it's mostly lost.

There was no backup. "Her erotic verse was thought to be
too scandalous by medieval scribes to save,"
and what we have—that snatch of tantalizing tatters
from "some trash pits near a branch of the Nile River"—
is dumb good luck. This, as opposed
to the earliest version we have of the *Iliad*
(still twelve centuries removed from its original composition)
—Homer's voice, turned into the first of the written versions . . .
and then a next . . . and then a next . . . until we have this
vellum manuscript from about A.D. 800, intact,
a surrogate with, by now, its own
earned aura of venerability. And so they had

their child—Danielle. She looked a little like Duane,
she looked a little like Annie. As these things go,
a perfect copy. Although for a sleepless week
she needed to be on life support: a curd of frail breathing,

in a robot tunnel of scanners and tubes. The second night there,
a storm muscled in, and the hospital's power failed.
What does eternity care, for any individual
grab-bag skin of us? What do the winds and the waters invest
in the flicker of protein structure that we call a life?
"Both Duane and I were in the ward, at her bedside,
when it happened. I swear: along with her, *our* hearts
stopped beating too." For a second. Luckily,
the backup electrical system kicked in.

4.

The history of the universe—
a dot. And then everything

exploding from the dot. And then a field
of expanding possibilitytrons

and eternacules, condensing and replicating themselves
into a stable system-state that's always itself

in every part of itself, and always
itself in reserve supply. It continues forever like this.

Eventually one arrangement of it is my father.
He's arguing, huff and puff, with a sixteen-year-old idiot

of a son whose hair is crazy long, whose life
is crazy friends and crazy music and crazy secular.

If only he could have lived to see me
sixty-one and staring into the mirror today

at exactly his face.

5.

And these are the intergenerational lines in *Genesis,*
after the Flood: Shem, Ham, Japheth, Meschech,
Gomer, Magog, Madai, Juvan, Tubal,
Cush, Tiras, Phut, Mizraim, Canaan, Eber, Elam,
Ashur, Lud, Arphaxad, Aram, Nimrod, and Tehrah;
for life is strategic and greedy, and it knows of the drouth
and the locust swarm and the sword, and it provides itself
with fallback DNA. And Terah was father unto Abraham;

and Abraham begat Isaac; and Isaac, Jacob;
and Jacob, Joseph: who was sold into bondage in Egypt
and there became the counselor of Pharaoh. And he saw
how there would be a time of plenteousness
for seven years, and seven years of famine thereafter.
And so he gathered up the corn without number; and when the dearth
came over the nations, in Egypt they builded the storehouses,
and there was bread. Those granaries functioning

as a shield against starvation: what the pickled squash
and salt-haunch must have meant to a Puritan family
as the winter shadows closed in on their village
like two hands around a throat. And yet for all

of his success—and he became the most powerful
man in the land, after Pharaoh—his secret dream might have been
to return to the shepherd rags of his youth. The secret dream
of the granary as it towers so imposingly there
against the carnelian sky of the Nile sunset . . .
might be waking as a simple toy,
"a granary" only about the size of a wooden whistle,
modest and sleek
and responsible for the pleasure of just one child.

6.

They squabbled. She was . . . "metaliferous," that's the word
he most often relied on: "Really, you don't want to curl up against
somebody who's all ore." And he . . . was like
a generalissimo of marriage: the invisible mustachios
of a second-rate grandee, the silly little invisible riding crop. . . .
And so Duane and Annie divorced. Of course by then
they'd each had other lovers stashed away
against this very circumstance—not unlike how
they'd stockpiled tins of vegetable slices and soup, and bottled water,
in the days when everybody feared "the millennium bug"
would blast us back to hands-on nineteenth century modes of living.
And anyway, by then the beloved Danielle
had said "fuck you" in a hundred different inventive
and hurtful ways, and run off to Vegas. She was sixteen,
and her dreams weren't theirs.

7.

I met her unexpectedly, when she was twenty-four and working
as a docent at a high-buzz exhibition of Etruscan art
at the Met. I hadn't seen her since . . . well, since
she was sixteen, some night of sudden dishes-hurling vitriolics
at their house.

              Now she was a woman of feline poise
and henna'd spikes. Inside, the statuary couples
on their sarcophagi lids accepted this revealing
twenty-first-century artificial light with a neighborly,
welcoming air. Outside, a block away, a hostage situation
had the cops blocking off our street . . . so we were stuck there
after hours, and could talk. The cops . . . reminding me
of that long-ago night when, probably, she was conceived. . . .
"My parents.

              What can I say? It was always my job
to look like her, to think like him, to be . . . like,
'Oh, we had a crummy day. But at least,
for a failsafe plan, we have Danielle tonight
to make us happy.' Right. The way you hear one day
we'll be able to harvest body organs from stem cells
—spares, like tires in trunks—to have on call
when needed. 'Oh, let's go get out Danielle.'"

                          It seemed
unfair; and accurate—both. We talked
of other things too. She was charming. I wished to stay
in her company, and for three more hours my wish was granted;
outside, sirens. The cops had called
for backup reinforcement. (Sometimes it helps,
and sometimes it doesn't.)

              As for the "Danielle" part,
"I'm Starr now"—had been, eight years. "What I needed
was a total break." Yes, but even so. . . .

"Last year, the directors let me assistant-curate a traveling show
on 'The Family Tree in Old Testament Days'—the way it turned out,
I knew more about the damn begats and the scholarship
than the big-freakin-deal emeritus fogeys in charge of it.
But of course. Go figure."

8.

I've seen them alluded to now
in so many poems . . . their candid, unrepentant sexual ease
and loving marital equity are qualities that seem to speak
convincingly across the gap of over two millennia
. . . these svelte and reclining Etruscan couples, shaped
to look as long and trim as otters sunning on a rock.
They seem to say that the olives are lush and piquant this year,
and the theater has never been better. They seem to say
that they were feeding olives to one another, fingers to lips,
just a moment ago, that the stone or bronze of their bodies
has a fluid, fleshy movement to it, and that we're invited
to join them, they who have been not only fortunate enough,
but conscientious enough, to be living in this contentedness
with legitimacy. Their perfect almond eyes and urbane smiles
surely say this. And the way their bodies fit the space
around them as smoothly as yolk fits white . . . this surely,
surely says it. But not their writing;
not to us. "This most elusive of dead tongues"*
is frustratingly untranslatable: we haven't yet discovered
a text that will help in unlocking the treasure. It's
as if (and I know logically that this isn't the case, but
it's as if) they've knowingly traded their chance to offer the world
translation backup, for this one
great golden moment.

---

* Nicholas A. Basbanes, *A Splendor of Letters*

9.

The cops succeeded, the street opened, Starr adjourned
to her office. I was left alone in the gallery for a handful of minutes,
before security hustled me toward the coat room.
I was alone—but I wasn't alone. And they told me,
It's good to have it,
the ace in the hole, the penny saved for a rainy day,
the stand-in waiting patiently in the wings
for when the star falls ill,
the silo against calamity. The disc
with international (hopefully, intergalactic) symbols
being floated out past the rim of anything knowable. Otherwise,
the ongoing is lost; and what does the universe ask
of its human beings, if not to be
both individual moments of power
and *components of a sequence? Now for us, in relation to you,*
in terms of language . . . the ongoing is broken.
We will never perform that duty. And you can call it a dereliction;
or you can call it an integrity
we keep, here, in our lives that haven't yielded
to transmission. It's always so complicated!
You have to go now—they're coming for you—you have to go out now
into the complexity. One day you'll be inert.
Not yet, not yet, not yet.

10.

Somebody's good luck is often somebody's
bad luck. It's always so complicated.
A man is skulking through the night. He has a need.
He's not a bad man, but he has a need
and he's going to fill it, one way or another. From a house,
upstairs, he hears the sounds of sex, and those involved in it
are on another world for now. It's dark,
but he can see, in the yard, a perfect example
of one of those plastic rocks that thoughtful homeowners use
as a backup: inside is the duplicate key.

The Blank

There are almost no facts about Theognis. His dates, his home city, the details of his life, and the authenticity of many of his poems are matters of scholarly controversy.

—DOROTHEA WENDER

Her name was Tara (hence the easy joke).
Was she the object of my old friend Rob's obsessive love,
one brief week since they'd first met on the Web?
—or just the object of his widely (also self-) acknowledged
obsessiveness purely? All I can report is that
I came across him mucking through her open purse
while she was gone one afternoon, in the middle
of seeking some telltale ribbon or stain,
a letter, a glittery splat of bijou, that
went a minor way toward fleshing out the unknown
who-she-really-was behind the charming surface
sexuality and lilting laugh. I never did forgive him this
betrayal of her trust (or just her unconcern?); and yet
who *doesn't* understand the need to fill the blank,

the teasing emptiness that's spooked us
and that's challenged us since "sky" and "dark" and, later,
"map" were emblems of its presence. If the cosmophysics gang
is right, and Universe and Mind evolve toward thicker
information-fields . . . well, like it or not, there Rob was,
doing his duty. And she *was* frustrating! On her Web site:
"I'm an orphan." Okay. "I work in cetacean biology."
Wow—impressive. And that was *it*. No further details.
Other men in her past? (or her present?) the places
she'd lived? her schooling? pets? pet peeves?
her secret naughty fetishes?—it was all absorbed
in a graceful shrug. As Sam, our reigning smartass queen
of weisenheimer shtick said, "What's her last name
—Incognita?" (Hey: I *told* you it was an easy joke.)

*Nobody knows for certain where or when Wordsworth and Coleridge first met,
what the circumstances were, or what was said.*

—ADAM SISMAN

"Here there be monsters" saith the ancient cartographers,
of unexplored terrain; they add depictions of the centaurs
and two-headed giants and artfully muscular-coiled dragons
inhabiting this X—a guess, the way our own string theory
is a guess, perhaps a bright guess and a best guess, but
a guess. And the ten-year-old girl is bored of doodling
her conjectures of what male-peepee must be like, she's
crazy for a real-deal look; and her eleven-year-old brother
sneaking enthralledly into the ladies room at Thinnegar's
Department Store one Sunday afternoon—the same.
And death is a blank, and what preceded Existence
is a blank: and so we conjure up a face for God,
we argue Big Bang yes-or-no . . . we doodle,
we wildly theorize, we hire P.I.'s. "An orphan

has it worst, I think." A year or so after
their breaking-up, I chanced on Tara (newly in town
to lecture at the aquarium), and we talked. "They died
in my first year. Maybe that's why I'm so stingy in giving
myself away—I have less of it than the rest of you."
Two other things I remember especially. "It's like a hole
in my history is physically present inside
my chest . . . like one of those runaway black holes from an experiment
they're afraid would gobble the world: it eats me more each day.
Maybe *that's* why I'm so dedicated to saving the river dolphin
from extinction . . . a hole I can fight against." And: "Rob
and the purse?" She laughed. "Oh you should see what *I've* done,
researching my parents." *Like . . . ?* "I'll only say a brick
through a window, and fucking several very creepy genealogists."

"An then 'e BOPS 'im over the 'ead an' TWISTS
'is shnozzle real friendly-like"—the first meeting
of Coleridge and Wordsworth, as interpreted by Monty Python.
Faceted, under the Cubist brush of Picasso, so the two
of them are set in the sylvan depths like humanoid crystals.
Elongated, by Modigliani. Winged, by Chagall. The truth
is, there's no truth. "Mystery surrounds 'Kubla Khan.'
No one can be sure exactly when it was written; no one
even knows whether it is complete. Coleridge
describes it as a 'fragment,' but there is a case
for doubting this." The truth is, choose to be kind
to another person, and let the rest of it go.
The truth is clouds and perishing and erasure.
Draw your own lines and hold firm. The truth is save

the Yangtze River dolphin, if it's not too late
to rescue that elegant blue-gray sinuosity
with the sweetly laconic grin threaded into its snout;
and it *may be* too late: "There hasn't been even one
confirmed sighting in six years," so the hope
of finding a breeding pair "has all but vanished."
The legend is a princess once refused to marry a man
she didn't love, and her angered family drowned her;
reincarnated into this spritely swimmer, she was known
now as "The Goddess of the Yangtze." Well, goodbye
to the goddess. Goodbye to the poems that Wordsworth
and Coleridge extemporized on their long walks. And the truth
is, Tara, we've failed your mission. One more hole
we'll need to halfass plug with some frantic invention.

Whether or not this story is true is a subject that has been endlessly debated, and can never be resolved, unless new evidence emerges. But of course that does not really matter.

—ADAM SISMAN

Sometimes a sensibility and a job are perfect matches;
in that way, Rob's obsessiveness—a trial
to friend and lover—has its culminant expression
as he's driven to fill in the fray and the flaking, here
in the bone-bare light of the art museum's restoration lab.
It's a pleasure to watch his thread-by-thread exactitude,
his grain-by-grain finesse. One day a missing eagle
is back in its mythological skies, is skimming above
the love-life of the gods for the first time in centuries.
Another day, a marble eye stares out of a marble face
once more. "Little voids: little patches." *And this?*
"I just finished them. Porpoises, we think. Right?
Aren't they porpoises?" And then an awkward silence
in which neither of us mentions her.

The dolphins that Theognis waxes so jubilant over
are oceanic, not freshwater; still, the familial
resemblance is strong. "Olympian Zeus, and the Daughters
of Inspiration, listen! In my seventh year, on a night
of the roundest moon, I went down to the shore
of the boundless sea, and there they were, those merry
children of Poseidon, leaping as if the water itself
had eyes and smiles and could leap. On one the moon
shone like a saddle, on her back, and indeed
I waded deeply in and she let me astride her,
and we circled the bay. This is true. I believed
she was mine and no one else's. There are wonders
in a life to be remembered." Although let me
confess here: I made that up. I couldn't bear the blankness.

"I taped a sign over the first sign"

—LOUISE GLÜCK

X-rays: we know Titian, in his *Venus With a Mirror,* included
originally a single male figure next to Venus who was later
painted out. And in a way, the history of painting—and especially
oil painting in the classic, layered manner—*is* a history
of coating over the trace of an earlier someone; as if art,
like evolution, has no pity for the buried,
and what we might say is revision
the Neanderthal would call genocide.

She'd modeled for him, a brainy and bosomy
undergraduate English major: *that* story. And then.
She weekly let her body make a body
of the morning light, she made it pour
like cognac, and she gave it the sugary potency
of a nectarine, and it seemed to him his new success
in galleries was half hers, and she stayed to talk
about her senior paper (Poe), and then, and joke
(her theories were poe-mo, she said), and then, and then,
and now.
                   It's night. *The dogs. . . .* It's ten years later and
it's night, and he appraises the work on the easel
—its continued refusal to finish right. The dogs / *his goddam
college friend Art Yaggerscheim* / keep baying,
long-drawn auditory versions of themselves
like a spectral pack on the hunt, and his college friend
who specializes in "concept art" and cutely signs his drivelproducts
"ArtY," so / *and he looks at her* / outsells his own
painstaking traditional portraiture by ten-to-one. . . . so many
burrs and diversions. Well, he yields
to nonaccomplishment for the day, rearranges
the brushes, and then returns to the house

from the studio. Her bedroom door is open
                                            and he looks at her . . .
whoever she is, by now,
a decade later. *That* story. Whoever she is,
she's asleep in her bed, in the dark there, under laminae
of unapproachability so thickly applied, that it
compares to ever-downward levels of the Hades-journey
separating Eurydice from Orpheus. He goes now
to his own room of the marriage—*that* interment.

These are people squirming some of the time
homuncularly in all of us.

But it isn't night

in Rembrandt's *The Night Watch.* That was our
misapprehension (and so misnomer) for all of those years,
until the "night"—the centuries
of coats of yellowed varnish and layers of dirt—
was cleared away, and the mustered neighborhood guard
(and the two little girls, and the boy, and the dog
he so often inserted gratuitously as a signature reminder
that life isn't all historic eminence and Biblical glory)
stand there in those newly revealed splashes of daylight
the artist directed around the composition (here, *kaboom!* and . . . here!)
at his impresario will. What was it like, for these people,
to be obscured in that gloom for so long? Like—

> worm inside the tequila murk
> original words of a palimpsest
> Atlantis at the bottom
> scaled thing and feathered thing inside ontogeny

~~super hero self inside of "secret identity"~~
~~a politician's conscience~~
~~the transexual's "me"~~
~~a trout in the hold of the waters~~

like—"He was very small
and there was too much fluid
and they couldn't hear his heartbeat."

—ROBERT HILL,
WHEN ALL IS SAID AND DONE

⇒⇐

*I was there, at the origin, beside her, in the way
that Lilith is there before Eve, and lollopped
the glistening tip of her tongue along Adam's
dawntime skin, and opened herself for the same
in return. I was there—with Venus. Need I say
any more?—with Venus! I was there. And then*

*the secondary version was applied, and paint
was set on my eyes like coins, and stuffed like
sausage into my gullet, and now I'm here,
still here, the way the useless legs are still
compacted in the whale, and the way at times
your shoulderblades remember their missing wings.*

⇒⇐

the blank panel
and then a layer of "size," the glue that was mixed
        with chalk or marble dust
and then the layer of imprimatura
and then the underdrawing

and then the grisaille
then sometimes a layer of glaze
Titian boasted of using
 "thirty or forty" glazes per painting

＞＝

subordinated:
not extinguished

"Before the late-blooming forebrain
can reason that the hiss we hear is
from an espresso machine,
the primitive amygdala whispers 'snake.'"

—GEORGE JOHNSON,
IN *SCIENTIFIC AMERICAN*

＞＝

She wakes up,

panics up, in the middle of night, a scream
packed halfway up her throat as solid as soil.
Coughs it out, then lets the sweat dry off. . . .
Again
the marriage / the dream / the herness of her. . . .
his inconsideration. . . .
He must still be in his studio, painting . . . meaning
what?—that she can locate *him* in her mind
more certainly than she can find her own occluded
who-she-is, that claws around
inside herself. . . . It doesn't help,
she thinks with a grin, a sick grin, that her favorite
Poe from oh-so-long-ago
is "The Premature Burial."

＞＝

"One is quintessentially alone in the self.
Everyone in the world is locked away
in a prison of one and held incommunicado."

—ERIC LARSEN,
A NATION GONE BLIND

there are bootprints
we left on the moon
and never returned
through all of the intervening years
of indifference and funding loss and know-how loss
to find again
I think of them as the most amazing
trilobite prints in the universe

   "One of the coolest things
about redoing old inner city apartments, at least
for me, is scraping the wallpaper off.
It's like being Leakey or Schliemann! In one I counted
eleven layers—eleven separate generations
of need . . . of declaration of independent taste.
You can scrape through an absolutely blank off-white
to a riot of parrots and jungle volcanoes.
I like to imagine I'm in the apartment below,
and I can hear different
footfalls of these people—what were their lives

like (or anyway not unlike)
the careful removal of strata of African rock
a tweezerpinch at a time
a dusted-off sliver of fleck at a time

until this rut is touched this afternoon
by sunlight as it was
the day these footprints were created
they're recovered now so perfect
every fold and point of pressure
we can see how the journey that led us
for a slake of water
or sheltering brush
began by stepping
out of the ape

"The single crime with which Picasso reproached himself . . .
was once during his early years of poverty in Paris
painting over a Modigliani canvas. Art historians
have repeated this effacement, methodically
neglecting the work of Modigliani."

—ARRANGED FROM DAVID B. MORRIS,
"EROS MODIGLIANI"

Jefferson, in a skittery cast of candlelight, at a desk,
describing the promise of a nation founded
on individual liberty and common cause . . . well
bubba and momma, *that's* history, *that's* flashes
from a dying dream—just check the morning paper
if you doubt it—so *that* civic scene becomes impasto'd over
with a muddy pall of blood-for-oil ick-gray, then
his early attempt at a heterosexual marriage (making
sure he isn't catty about it or too regretful, allowing
this sketch of Flo to show her dignity and admirable

cheekbones)—*that* drowns under a thick gray goo,
and then his ancient one-time friendship
with the sanctimonious Pasha of Ho-Hum Portraiture,
that gets its cakey layer of opacity, and now
the surface is solid black, or what's
a "concept painting" *for?*—and wow, he's all jazzed up now,
he's electric, he just *loves* the background yowling
of those dogs that adds another, extra
texture to the whole act, and they suddenly remind him
of the dog that scoots from some world
out of the frame and into so many of Rembrandt's otherwise
officiously glorious constructs . . . so, for nothing but
the spirited ArtY-signature-gesture hell of it,
he adds in the corner a small stick figure
of Banning Cocq, the captain of that company
of musketeers, who's clambering—like a fly
from a paddy of blackberry jelly—out,
or *almost* out, of that iconic
but erroneous night.

———

like—
~~the mob boss's hit list, stuffed in a pillow~~
   ~~(doesn't it ever trouble his dreams?)~~
~~the society matron's past as an exotic dancer~~
      resse memo
~~a sunken galleon~~
  repre   morie
~~a trout in the hold of the waters~~
~~a fetus that dies in utero~~
      pressed emories

———

Sometimes the waggly buggish-visaged aliens emerge
like a coin—a terrible wish—that's gagged back up
the stone throat of the well. Hypnosis can do it,
or a "sudden shock." It's never happened to me.
But to some. A knock at the neocortex,
from the stem. A little hello to noon,
from midnight—after all, they were identical
in the womb. For a year, for twenty years,
that minute in the coat room,
in the basement, in the back of the abandoned bowling alley,
is forgotten; the chants and the circle of scarlet candles
and the chains—forgotten. Dormant. Exed.
~~the bear in the cave~~
So far as I know, I don't have any
voices attempting to scream out their existences
from my molten core. Some do. Some suffer
surface quakes—the voices asserting autonomy.
And even so ~~the ashes in the urn~~
~~the girl in a swaddle of everybody's inattention~~
I can't bear to think of the cowardly way I broke
the news to Sylvia, *hammer it down,* or remember my father
when he opened the door to find me masturbating, *hammer it*
into a powder, into one dense anti-atom of powder
in a gyroscope at the center of the Earth.
Somebody's multiple personalities.
Somebody's song in the wooden jaws of a marionette.
I think of the earlier, formal, more derivative poems
of Adrienne Rich . . . on top of them, a fecund, burning sod
of her feminist effort. Once,
the moon was inside of the Earth.
The Earth was inside of the radiant energy
of the universe before there was mass,
before there was "direction" enough for "orbit" to be

a concept. On a day like this, I'm walking
through my neighborhood aware of every life
in every house as a revision of something, *someone,*
predecessory. If I walk until night, in some room
there's a nude, elastic, ruby-hued
Modigliani woman waking into the tarry darkness
of her exile under Picasso's suppressive
application of paint.
She yawns, she stretches . . .
slim and cool and risen now visibly
like a trout from the hold of the waters.

A PREMISE AS TOUGH AS MONOGAMY

"An enormous electro-magnet is used to steal the world's electricity"

—PLOT SUMMARY OF A 1925 NOVEL IN A CATALOGUE
OF "CLASSIC FANTASTIC LITERATURE"

Elsewhere, drowned Atlantis is found (populated;
powered by a "mystic jewel of Issus") with less
difficulty than you've endured in searching
for your car keys. Elsewhere, isotopes of "flightium"
allow a locomotive-looking "sky ship" to ascend
to Mars: it turns out that the lost (←no longer) tribes
of Israel live here now, in grandiose enclosures
underground, beneath those strings of roseate lesions
on the surface—it's a narrative that mixes
sober Pentateuchal sweep with the pulpier world
of space age brawls and gutsy space age femme fatales.
Elsewhere, an immortality pill. Elsewhere, attack
by martial "lizard men" is foiled by "magnetic coil
thruster beams" a rogue inventor cooks up in a tipsy spree.
These stories test, or are, the distant edges of belief;
although inventing a credible sunrise in a Minnesota
small town on a winter day in 1948 . . . its orange fingers
on the lake ice, and the human lives this light awakes
in touching them: the quietly expectant,
and the fearful, the fatigued . . . is no less category "fiction"
than some sun that sends out zooming fleets of alien invaders
to our town. The heat of each is equally real
(or equally dubious). In the catalogue of "naturalistic
twentieth century fiction," in the houses of growing up
in Newkirk, Catiesville, Lake Ketchawan,
the difficult lessons—and also the wonders—are plentiful,
on the journey to something so galactically far away
as womanhood or manhood. In a country just done dealing
with the holocaustal touch of World War II, a couple
labors to believe, still, in a monitory God

whose will is basically benign; and elsewhere, say
in Northern Corners or in Endersburg, another couple
works to believe, oh works so hard
across a plot as long as a life, to simply believe
in a premise as tough as monogamy.

Hard Pope

"Galileo was not absolved of heresy until 1992."

—SAM HARRIS

It was like that—a little. I know it *seemed* to be
four hundred years. But I wouldn't forgive her.
Not in a night, and not in a week of nights, and not
in time that might be measured even in lengths
of hibernation and master migratory patterns. I was iron,
the weeping didn't exist under which I was biodegradable.
And every night this thundercloud of anger was my will;
and every morning, her inheritance. And when that storm
had spent itself torrentially . . . its residue ire continued
to drip from the leaves. The Paleozoic passed, a lizard
sunning itself on a flat rock moved at last, the rock
itself was finally moved in a yawn of the planet's crust, but
not me—not my heart, it wasn't moved
toward expiation by so much as a caraway seed, no,
not by a single unit of neurotransmitter. It's a fact
that to perform a glorious music, a person needs to fill
the spit valves of his cornet; well, my indignation thought
of itself as a glorious music: I spit on her apology,
on the interior will she bent in a salaam.
I withheld. The Stone Age passed, but not the stone of me.
I withheld, I was mountainous no, for what was
(in emotional equivalency-days) the full 2,000 years of darkness
in a Japanese tomb before the seed they discovered in there
in 1992 was planted and flowered into the mazey folds
of a white magnolia. Galileo—did he care, wherever he was
for all of those centuries? Now, for us, it's difficult enough
to imagine his life—he's like a little plastic figure
for a toy train village, studiously squinting through his telescope
or lecturing the inquisitors sent by the Church; how much

more difficult to see him in his dormancy beyond the grave,
as he waited for Rome to finally catch up with his universe.
With others, of course, there is no wait for a recognition
of innocence . . . but who would desire the terms of *that?*
"The Spaniards in Peru and in Mexico
used to baptize Indian infants and then, right after,
dash their brains out, thus securing them an immediate
station in Heaven"—they were unstained
by the musks and the salts of living.

Through the Elements

Outside now, a heavying sleet; the milo
hanging its thousands of heads
like a field of penitents bent to their punishment.
Nothing stops this wrath from coming down

to lay its cold pelt on the body of the world.
It's less like weather and more like an enemy army
billeted here, for as long as it chooses.
Nothing stops this iron wind, or stops us

from confusing it with the other enormous severities
in our lives we can't control—our rage
and the incomprehensible rage of others, our covetousness,
the voices of reproach that fill the dark

beyond all reconciliation; "I can pour this in
all night," a woman told me once, with a high-held
bottle for proof, "and still wake up
with my soul as dry as a stick." And so I understand

our retreat to the worlds of our expertise
and their buttressing jargons: semiotic studies,
or those lustrous rows of nymph lures at the bait shop
(tasseled like wheat and bangled like harem dancers,

as pure in their colors as iodine or bananas).
The phlebotomist has his, the endocrinologist
hers. And here, in this arcana, we consolidate
the self. For every given jurisdiction,

its own lingo and its magistrate in charge.
Somebody owns a Kevlar vest, somebody knows the odor
of vernix flowering off the skin. The merkin. A foley.
Isotope geochemistry. The czardasz. "Bryophytes," as Bryson

puts it, "—mosses to the rest of us." It's almost two
in this small-town bar, and the rest of us
are reluctantly bundling up to hunch on home
through this assault of chill and damp. Now even

Mr. Loquacious Attorney is out the door,
then Ms. Pool Hustler, with the aura of their respective
vocabularies and secret signs about to flicker
and dim in the harsh air. Now—it's after three—

the bartender and his stripper girlfriend finally lock up,
shouldering their way like a Great Plains herd of two
through the elements. Oh . . . excuse me.
The mixologist and the ecdysiast.

Beauty

In the earliest twentieth century—when the art was new
enough to affront and harangue and bamboozle—
the Russian millionaire Sergei Shchukine saw it,
truly *saw it,* through prophetic, empathizing eyes:
Cezannes, Gaugins, Matisses, tiered
upon the walls of his palatial home in Moscow,
each a vibrant contribution toward a connoisseur devotion
indistinguishable from love. Although after
the Revolution, the state took over the house
and the art in its own name, and Shchukine
was ordered to serve there as a guide
to his former collection. He might have thought he saw
this story in one of the paintings, one of the many
beckoning nudes. The woman's husband, who had once
possessed her thoroughly—each minute;
every taste of her—has been cuckolded now.
And even so, he welcomes current lovers at the door,
and will not turn his eyes away, or renounce her.
Who is Shchukine to say that
beauty isn't worth it?

Tool

What isn't? Even as the child
attaches a hook to the string of his homemade pole,
the water of the pool is busy
bending light. The moon
bends light. The child bends
the life-arc of its parents.
We register gravity and
we register resistance. When I look
at my wife beside me in bed, it helps me
see myself. We're substance
dropped into time, to measure its flow.

"Snowflakes unnumberably come down."
—a line from Howard Nemerov. A pleasure
to see the language used
so expertly, with a kept-sharp edge.

My father always said to clean
and resharpen them after every use.
That was *his* way . . . thoroughness,
practical care. Easy now
to remember him unstiffening the paint from a brush,
a bristle at a time, below the running faucet.
Not me. Just look at the strew, the clutter-dump,
I call "the back seat of my Nissan."
It was like the air between us,
like the ligature of father and son
between us: he kept his side of it
in gleaming, working order, and I . . .
I polished up my side of it
for the funeral, it had to come to such rust.

It's sometimes also a wonder to watch
the misuse. Michael one day with an ailing tree
and a chain saw. Its refusal, its so very close
to conscious, refusal to start—one time, twice,
twenty. And then the sudden tommy-gun rocketing
out of his hands that, on its own, as if a garden sprite
controlled it, in a matter of seconds
demolished the dog house roof. Up in the tree,
a bird efficiently used a twig to wedge a seedcase open,
studied us with a brisk hauteur,
then showered down laughter. Unnumberably.

The hammer. The adze. The hoe. The looking-up
of tools on doubleyoudoubleyoudoubleyoudottoolsdotcom,
and so using the hand, or the voice command,
and the flurrying imps of the Internet.
The supermicrofiber that enters the kidney's
swampy conduits is a tool, of course, but if
you believe in it so is the parents' prayer.
We can make a shadow a tool.
We can trepan. We can titrate.
What are *these* marks?—well, for twenty years
my wife and I have each attempted to shape
the other one to what was perceived
as the marriage's needs. Sometimes, it's true,
the results have been beautiful and consoling. Sometimes *hey
that HURTS.*

The eye can't see itself.
The tongue can't taste itself.
And so we require a tool for this,
even one so faulty as love.

Signed On

The Science-Fiction Book Club wants you! In fact, the Club will send you at once—absolutely free—an authentic Moon tour Reservation. This wallet-size Reservation certifies that you are among the first to apply for such a trip, but does NOT commit you to actually take the voyage.

—MAGAZINE AD, 1958

1. Thank God for the loophole; otherwise . . .

3 in the morning; a loud determined knock on the door / (hesitantly) "Who—who is it?" / (curt, no-nonsense) "Open up, sir." / "Who is it?" / "The SFBCEP. Open up." / "Who?" / "The Science Fiction Book Club Enforcement Patrol. Open up. We can show you ID." / (the door cracks open slowly on a chain, ID is slipped through and consulted, and then—not without an understructure of rising panic—a man in pajamas opens the door to two large, burly men in tough-guy nondescript black trenchcoats) / "Please. Please tell me what this is about?" / "You recognize this, sir." / (this is a statement, not a question; a wallet-size card is in one man's hand) / "Well, no, I don't. No." / "This *is* your name? Your signature?" / (he studies it more closely) / "Uh . . . yes. Yes, it is, but. . . . Why, this card is from my childhood. I remember! I was ten . . . yes, fifty years ago. How wonderful! Where did you. . . ." / "Please pack a bag as quickly as possible, sir." / (confused; almost dazed) "A bag?" / "With enough to see you through to station one of the journey, sir. You're off to the moon." / "To *what?*" / "To the moon, sir. You're committed—let me repeat: committed—to take that voyage." / *"What?"* (backing away) / "This Reservation *is* signed by you sir. We don't want to use force unless necessary."

2. And so that's the story of Jack and Mimi

—only without the comedy,
the book club, and the spaceship waiting
magnificently in its silver dock at the port.
The lunar presence, however, *is* here with them:
its fullness—its immense gold ripeness—
drives their seventeen-year-old hormonally-revving bodies
into an hour of furtive, fumbling-but-unerring
grope-and-open pleasure under the Oak Street viaduct
one August night, so simple an act, so common
a result, that we can follow its tear-tracks,
gritted teeth, and screams like footprints into the future:
pregnancy; the shackling, too-soon marriage;
the mortal eternity of diapers-and-snot (for her),
of a life on the burnishing line at Titan Electric (him);
the death of a dream, the death of options . . . it's as if
the needs of DNA and the dictates of nuclear family culture
met one day in a boardroom and connived
to bring her down here, with a seventh beer, to the gravel lot
at the end of the block tonight, to feel the gravel-spill
that everything inside of her has turned to, and to stare up
through her blurred gaze to the silvery sickle-edge that hangs
above her in the sky, and to mutter repeatedly her little mantra
Mimi, mommy, mummy, like the stages of her self
from its spring to its autumn. Who'd have guessed
how in that hour under the viaduct they'd signed on
for the whole lifelong inevitable excursion?
It could also be a commitment to a creed, or an art, or
. . . anything, really. These two are anthropic:
you could seed them into a petri dish and grow
the rest of us overnight. You think you don't know
Jack and Mimi? Ah. If so, it must be
that you don't have neighbors. You don't have friends.

3. *But there* are *more clement outcomes*

—sometimes. Maybe. If the brains and hearts
that serve as dice get rolled that way. If not,
then not. As for those early and ordinary
misgivings about the marriage, that I felt "suffocated,"
"chained" (presumably she did too), and then resultant
"backlash," any anger, any light-but-constant
leashlike chafe that served as an excuse to bring up
sundering the bond . . . all that was true. And yet
the years went on, and maybe it was trust
or maybe lethargy, the years went on, however a poem
might put it—a jumble, a turning celestial wheel,
a millrace, of ongoing years—with all of the world's unstopping
tabloid gossip, blogspeak, military intel, and the other
hundred fracas-voices and -vocabularies blipping in
and out . . . *if greenhouse gas emissions / stint in rehab*
(why is it always a "stint"?) / a tiny drop of oil of wintergreen
on her tongue-tip first / autistic/ toxicology, and they kept it
in a canister called the tox box / ultraviolet / pollarded /
systems theory / forced at gunpoint / alpha dog
and bottom dog / whoa / eremitic desert fathers / trashy
halter-tops the colors of urinal cakes / election fraud /
in guano / teleology / whoa / through a mind long bitter
with ruth / results not typical / folderol / whoa I said WHOA . . .

and on the other side I awoke, I looked at my wife
beside me: she was beautiful, the way the passing time
had smoothened her and roughened her. I slipped from bed
and walked into the yard of this place—and not only
a physical place—where we could live apart
from the planet a little. It was truly an astonishing light
that fell into the yard from the sky . . . as if

the leaves could slice it, into something shining
on the one side and, on the other, profoundly dark.
How far had we journeyed to get here, I'd often wondered.
And now I understood. I was on the moon.
And I was happy.

TOWARD (AND AGAINST) THE FUTURE

To Be Read in 500 Years

*To think of today . . . and the ages continued
henceforward.*

—WALT WHITMAN

She bring me love love love love, crazy love.

—VAN MORRISON

If they're right, the whizkid physicist-theorist thinktank guys,
suggesting that every acted-on decision of ours produces a brachiation
in the timestream (therefore, two simultaneous independent futures:
for example, one extending from my use of "brachiation,"
one extending from my *almost*-use of "fork," so that
tomorrow-"b" and tomorrow-"f" are equally real in parallel
and coexistent tracks), there may be, secretly among us,
a few—or even entire populations—of backward travelers
in time from not just one, but many, "alternamorrows,"
so different from ourselves, it's like the thought that bitch-ho' rap
and the sublimities of, say, Chopin are kin enough to both be
reproduced by variant patterns within the same 88 keys:
                                                      in one
of these futures, everything essential, every attribute of humanness
even minimally desirable, is relegated to mind alone
—we look like cumulonimboid dendrite-structures
that have flowered out of small deflated flesh-pods—
and the reproductive function of the species now
is entirely exocorporal, a matter of frozen protein combinations
and gestation-sacs of complex bioplastic;
                                              in another
of these futures—it's an after-we-squander-the-oil-deposits world
of post-apocalyptic, bare-subsistence living—a day
is a matter of thinning, granular soil: leached,
defiant of yielding to our human need and its desperate threshing

—that, and a rumor from over up north that dog troops
of marauding goons are on the march with pillage and worse
asquirm in their eyes—and there, and then, all softness,
all of anything without "survival value," has been bred out
of the race, so "interpersonal relationship" is no more
than a reflex of the genes;

                              or, *au contraire,*
another future makes an ornate, public fetish of the wooing game
—a codified fantasia of modes of address and rank and dowry
and clan and feather-on-cloak-by-depth-of-genealogy, etc.—
to a social architecture of such overmuch extent that, while it's all
intensely focused on the establishing of a betrothal-pair, it's
all at the same time so bound up in duty and cultural sanction
as to be even more devoid of anything personal—anything soulful
and open to flutter—than the future I've described
of petro-aftershock . . .

                              and therefore *none* of these baffled representatives
encamped in our twenty-first century can understand,
can "get," the thump, the cupid-zing, the woe and the wow,
in our songs and poems, especially the songs, especially the glowing
uranium dump that malingers all night at the bottom of the blues,
oh especially the blues, especially let her light shine down
on me, especially by the waters of Misery Avenue, let's not forget
Heartbreak Hotel, let's not eschew its transient cast
of cinders-and-ashes clientele, but also the songs of tra-la-la
and marital abidingness, of how sometimes a body fits a body
as indivisibly as waves (or it could be particles) fit light, the poems
address this too of course, the let me count the ways, the roses
in their fragrant and meaty botanical abundance, and the doves,
let's not forget the doves, the old thou art a summer's day
and thy breasts are of wheaten beauty, let's not dillydally in recognizing
the wedding under the laws of God, let's not exempt the quickie
under the snooker table, the flame in the bones, the one name drummed

in a bruising tattoo on the heartskin, they don't comprehend this sugartit thing,
this sonnet thing, this sky held in the mirror pools
of the Taj Mahal on a day of slowly promenading couples
thing, these people of the future as I've imagined them don't have
the apparatus of leisure we've had, in a special lotus of time
that's been vouchsafed to us, a mythos, a sequestering in which
this serotonin and this opium are grown to a lyric degree, they wouldn't
understand me sneaking out at 5 a.m. to pat that ten-dollar valentine
tenderly into place beneath the wiper-blade of Phyllis's swayback Dodge
(with the fishtaily brakes and the fanlight crack in the windshield), they
don't know the drive-in, the down at the corner, the boardwalk, the bridge,
the places where it happens and where we commemorate it, also a night
of blind and driven howling I pulled like an hours-long ebony scarf
from the deeps of my brain-stem once on Morgan's lawn, so sweet
it is, this ineluctable thing, this please let one of the harder sciences objectify
the biochemical basis of our here-do-that-to-my-earlobe-another-time
thing, down by the riverside, at the gates, behind the stadium,
and Skyler my wife with the basement tiles and cowboy pajamas,
she lift me up, she bring me the dominions of the morning
and the thrones of the moon, they've never once experienced this
impossible night of her wanting him down to the vitamins
and the pepsin and the aura and the spit, and how she bring him
the molasses and the escrow and the skidmarks and the holy church,
the rock and the water, the star and the stain, together we heard
the otherworld hosannas of wind in the alders, not to mention
karaoke screech, the Gregorian chant and the triple-X rebel yowl,
it requires a certain coddled recipe of history and maybe economics
and the industry they generate, the castles and the sly décolletage,
I wanted to read her the works of Montaigne and Cervantes and Emerson
and I wanted to slip her some tongue, I was enrolled, I stayed
the course from my first day in Agony 101 to my post-doc, they will never
be burned by this ice, they will die without knowing the thirst
in this river, she bring me the spackle, she give me the flying tackle,

he build her up, he tug her plug and she drains, she becomes
a puddle of ouch, she hit me with the hoodoo, with the magic spell
and the candle, they will never know this candle, yeah
she lead me up the towpath got a diamond in my nose, she dress
in ermine and sable, she barefoot in the grass, I tossed,
I thought of words like chivalrous and serenity, I spied on her,
I wanted to kill for her, she bring me the cherry wine, the toxic waste,
the whole wheat and the half-shell, they will never eat of this fruit
and suffer its consequences, never beg for its juice, its family root,
she be my guide, she interlocutor, my Beatrice-*and*-Virgil (and me behind
in my Dante sandals following her shake-that-thing on the stony path),
my rash, my silty unguent, she rob him, she rock and throb him,
she greet him in his guise as the charioteer of the sun in its vast
celestial passage, in the centuries forthcoming they will never know
this honeycomb of confusion and its confected delight, it happens
in the jazz bar, at the casbah, in the synagogue, under the sheets,
she lift me higher, she be my desire, she build me, she give me,
in the sand dunes, hot hot summer, on the roof, yes here, now here,
a little lower, she feed me, she give me, she lift me, she need me,
the sound of the continents as they first tore apart and the surge of the oceans,
the music of that, the songs especially but also the poems, she take me,
the rosins of craving, the tables of lust in its periodicity, they cannot
and cannot and cannot partake of this feast and the terrible emptiness
that follows, she make me, she lift me, I freely give her one grand opera rose
and hiphop dove, she under my skin, she knife in my mind, this thing,
oh this millennial and hallucinatory and radiant thing, she bring me,
she lift me, she take me, she bring me love
love love love crazy love.

The Sword

This was the feeling his friends all shared:
that it was over. Reading was over; if not, then
anyway reading *as a willed and private and pleasureful act
that helps shape a culture* was over. This was exactly
the way they emphasized it. And privacy itself
was gone: the cams in public squares, the admitted
tracking of citizens' phone calls. Surely decorum
was over: all of that "reality TV" in celebration
of our most whorish selves. And the oceans,
and the atmosphere: it was over. Under our insufficient
stewardship, they were altering at the molecular level
in irreversible ways. And after oil was depleted, then
everyday safety was over, and we could return to the age
of the club and the feral street dog. Everything was over,

almost. That was the key word. They were the last; and this,
the Era of Almost. He could see it
on this winter day when he stopped for some warmth
at the art museum . . . there, in floating color where
a single tree against the orange light was like a tendon,
like a structure, that implied a place
and a narrative: in this case, "autumn hills": it was the tree
that enabled our seeing the orange as "light," and its gradations
as a sense of continuing landscape. If those few lines
were withdrawn. . . . He went back out. Already the wind
was personal, it wanted to see him brace. The sky
was a heavier gray. It was snow overhead, enough
to slay the city. For now it waited up there:
ready, but still sheathed.

Unformed

We read our idea of "childhood" back
into the figures in paintings from before the concept existed:
look at the blandly middle-aged faces
—sad old thumbs—on the children in Breugel's
The Census at Bethlehem, 1566. They're on the ice
in something like the attitudes of winter play,
but the shoulders-first push of their blocky bodies
against this hard gray air, and those eyes like mouse scat
left in a plate of gruel . . . these say exactly
the difficult adult labor of the butcher
slicing a gush of pig blood out of that animal's ropy throat,
or Joseph bowed below the heavy carpentry saw
across his back as he leads his pregnant wife
on the pack-beast over the crusted snow. Those

children . . . they won't, not for centuries, grow
into the ones around us everyday, with their own
specific clothing and terrors and needs, the years
will have to drop into Rousseau's unexpected theories like seeds
before they can flower into latchkey programs,
orthodontia, Toys-R-Us. Nor will *our* faces seem
complete to the future, whatever it's like, whatever
ability it has to nanobot a failing spleen or sculpt
the shoulders into opened wings or register the thought
of a field of bluegrass, or whatever its brutal willingness
to kill on sight: we're almost there, but not there,
and our faces are unformed as yet: the blank and stale
eggs that, up until just a handful of months ago,
Mary's body would have flushed out of itself.

Into Blossom

*Of course we still love the idea of books, but we have an ever harder time
tooling down to engage them as they were written to be engaged. Which is
to say slowly, linearly, with single-track focus. Ours is now a world of high-
speed action and reaction, of necessarily distributed awareness, of layered
simultaneous involvements.*

—ARRANGED FROM AN ESSAY BY SVEN BIRKERTS

The Rapture, or a kind of Rapture, is going to come
and lift us with its claws in our nape or our waist-fat
(this is why "rapture" and "raptor" are cousins); or it
will take us the way that Zeus did Leda or
God did (fill in any one of the calendar's swooning
heart-speared saints); or, more to my current
purposes, it will land and say "welcome aboard"
as understood (in one of a hundred different languages
preprogrammed according to retinal scan) by an ever-ready
installachip behind our eyes, and we will take our place inside
that cybergenetic condor-jet-amalgam sensurround-vehicle,
and it will whoosh us away to the land of multistreaming screens
with neuro-plug-in capability, it will fly us across
an everyday hill of oak and scattered stone, and abruptly
into the vectors of info-boom and synchro-loop, oh it will whoosh us

—most of us. As for me, I'm sitting here pleasurably
with my back against one of those oaks. I can feel
the pattern of its bark—like Persian lamb—moiré my back.
The sun is out. A fly is insistent. I'm reading a poem
of James Wright's, on a printed page: I'm doing
nothing else. He's patting a horse now. He's breaking,
he says, into blossom. I'm small and quiet and rapt.

The Mailbox

"Ninety percent of all the scientists who have ever lived are alive today. They are developing new knowledge at a rate that will double every 10 years."

—U.S. GOVERNMENT INSTRUCTIONAL BOOKLET, 1963

1.

The billboard: sex:
her zingy strap of spandex pusher-upper
is a shelf for the display of museum-quality mounds
of a bodily tiramisu, while the male model mows
straight off his lawn and up his front porch steps,
in ogling her. And in the drier but equally
beguiled deeps of the *Catholic Diocese Manual for Couples
Undergoing Recommended Counsel Prior to Marriage:*
sex. In the laundromat: sex. In the cave. The synagogue.
The principal's office. In the plane of the man who charges
an hourly rate to pilot frisky couples circumspectly
into a high canoodling. Even the ten-year-old is aware
of her burgeoning power; she can sense the room
conform to her, already she can dream of an empire shortly
doing the same. On the Web: oh surely and technomanifoldly
everywhere on the Web. In the intricate lithic writhe
of Indian gods on a jungle-creepered wall. A man
and his wife. A man and his room of a thousand
dirty pages. Somewhere in the convent,
in the flagellant's cell, at the chastity pledge, somebody
is not and is not and is not and is never
thinking of sex—this too is sex's power, this is the sucker wallop
and the wonder and the totalitarian reign of DNA.
Tonight in the garden too: under a scrabble of stars
and, just before it disappears altogether, a peach-pit moon.
The flowers are laxly-widening budoir yawns.
The insects are sexual engines

without a break. And the other domain is here
as well: I come across the broken-open body of a cardinal
being disassembled by maggots, so many
they look like a single paste at work, a dissolvent
that faintly smells of bowel, and will not stop
its feeding until there's nothing
but a few bone spindles left on the soil.
From in the house . . . some mediababble . . .
silicon nano-imaging studies . . . superconductor antiparticles . . .
giga-information clones. . . .
                              As if it weren't more than enough
to be out here with the old knowledge.

2.

Here's a premise for a science fiction story. In the world
of tomorrow, we produce an android
intended to aid us in exploring
other planets. This is its wired-in capability:
this manufactured being who looks exactly like us
can enter and comprehend and be imprinted by
the mind of an alien life-form (only one
at a time—but one in the totality
of its otherness, its up-until-this-moment
indescribably foreign knowledge, is surely a scientific
miracle enough). And this knowledge is emptied
into a special neurocomputer storage bank
—it's called the "datatorium"—and our android now
is clear, and ready to meet and be congruent with
his next assigned alien consciousness.
It works without a hitch, on the planet of sand toads
in their smart and monkish existence, on the planet
of sentient mist, the planet of banshee things.
The breakdown comes on a planet where—and no one
had foreseen this—we discover a communal mind,
so just the one encounter overloads our android hero
with a kind of palimpsest-effect that can't
be halted now or controlled, and knowledge after knowledge is added
in layers, and then in annexes
and helter-skelter wedged-in jams where previously
a clarity, or at least a pretense of clarity,
had been present. Now the plot goes
—where, from here? He becomes like a superhuman,
a god? He implodes? He finally solves the question
that the universe is? He runs berserk, he gibbers?
Can you imagine it? I mean that: *you.*
Right now: can you imagine it?

3.

So often (let's be honest here) we poets
will *invent* dreams, for our own strategic purposes.
But this one is real, and one of the few
I remember. I awoke in the future.
What the mechanism was, I never knew;
but I awoke whole and feeling no different.
The sky was clear, the day was sunny, the scenery
parklike. I was met by a congress of friendly
academic types, and although they were dressed
familiarly in tweedy jackets and rumpled ties—nothing
aerodynamic or cyberfibered, for example—it was clear
by dozens of subtle and inarticulable signifiers,
a century or more had gone by. And so I was
important to them—a Man of the Past! They led me
toward their university grounds: I was given the sense
I was to be studied, but as an honored guest.
Meanwhile they chatted, they pointed out this and that:
a glassy tower of opaque purpose,
a large self-gardening lawn. Little marvels
—enough for me to gasp, and yet easy enough
to accept. But I realized, after a while of this
eavesdropping on their gab, that they didn't have books
any longer . . . and when I asked, they laughed, as if
I'd just asked if they churned their own butter.
Paper—did they have paper? And where were the libraries?
Did they have libraries, still? Music, still?
The printing press? And why it should come down to this
I don't know, but I noticed
there were no mailboxes along their curbs. And suddenly
a feeling of such immense loss flooded over me . . .
I didn't yet know what had happened to "love"
or "cancer" or "war" or "philosophy"

or "corporation" or "family" or "art,"
but I was weeping—I woke up
weeping—over "mailbox."

And the sight of one is a pang to this day,
December 5, 2006.